THE GIIIRL IN THE ORANGE DRESS

(mumblings from within)

ED BREATHE

Copyright © 2023 by Ed Breathe

All rights reserved. No part of this book may be reproduced or used in any manner without written permission of the copyright owner except for the use of quotations in a book review.

978-1-80227-430-1: eBook
978-1-80227-431-8: hardcover

Contents

Pea-Ce 8
FAail.InG aGAain 9
A strange sensation 10
FeeeeeT 11
StAt U 12
Fri End 13
bEst Fri. End fLo 14
BRe -AK 16
Breaa. THE BreAtH 18
I's 20
Lu Na 21
fLoAAAAAAAt+ingG 22
ThO SSEEEE 24
Cl OsE 26
hAaapy dAze 27
Wat-Er Of LIiiFe 28
ScREEN(m) ed out 29
FiSH Sing 30
MAD SHADOWS 32
Stu nnnd 34
WHol es 35
THOug.HT-s 36
Piii Geons IN My FrrrIDge 38
tHe Flig/Ht 40
SUN 42
BEaaaaan ZZ 43
Imp eriaL PINT 46

OLd R age (wiLl Owe) 48
tHe JoUr Knee 50
ThE PaSs I oN 51
LloSs-T hOPe 52
R Eeeeliza-Be Th 54
sPeEeeeEed 56
wiNDsoF.ChAIN-g 58
ThE giRrrrRrlL 60
Lo(o)CKUp 61
pAthW ay 62
Re Ach oUT 63
10 Y Ears AftA 64
Po(och) rEturn 65
In Tens e 66
In Die an 67
EdGEs 68
iNfiNi 69
The GIIIIRL IN THE OrAnge DRESS 70
thE PrIOr (y) 72
Re FLeX io=n 73
Four BiDDeN 74
D/ US /t 75
ShoE t Boy HOOD 76
Tri-Um-Ph 77
T He Aaad/VerT 78
FiNaL iTy 79
AbYss 80
GGiraaaaaFfE LaaaauGH 82
BlAaaCK AnD Why-te? 84
B R 86
He At 87

GEnntlE -MeN TIIiiiiime!	88
Faaal eN	90
StrUCTural CoLLaPse	92
SYLPh	94
ThE Lo-VeR	96
Dream InG SunS	98
Com Fort	100
HeRe WE aRe Again	102
Old AGe (Wil Owe)	104
Hunt [er]smoon	106
Chinewrde	108
sPIT 110ire	110
Look Back	112
The table	114
TAKe & giVe	116
2–0: five	118
sTOrm	122
gUArd-Aeons	124
Kill (we're all going to die)	126
pLOt	128
mIN d	130
¼ TET	131
PlAn it Rape	132
riVeR of ObLiviiion	134
bRid(g)e	136
Un Said	138
PLAs-sTiCK	140
69/77	141
Going Undr	142
Spy derr	144
My Fri END	146

The (f)EAR	148
Ass UMP tioN	149
A Bad dAY	150
lOsT HOpe	151
De'aths door	152
s-LasH of rED	155
CuP Bored	157
WIN ter	158
rOOT	159
F-EAT (2)	160
T(hE)M	162
Shdw	163
bAL-a-NCe	164
close	165
sEA GIrL	166
Amen	167
aN vIL	168
eNd of The liNe	170
HOPE	172
thE 200,000	173
cORt	174
Con fuse shun	175
The 5 year old	178
lOst at The CafE	180
T-emp-eST	181
Z s(HeLL) ter	182
WaVe Early	184
4041 STAR	187
20 fOUR tHOU (sand)	188

1

Pea-Ce

A simple peace of frozen sunsets
Draws the eye into the place where we've wandered
Pondering a fate that waits in the wings to reveal the life that makes us sing.
Heads are down, back to the sun, we stare at earth from which we come
The seeds we sow, though some will die, some give rise to bright new life
That lets us fly to cloudless skies, to set us free and wonder why.

Oh, why we didn't look up before? What kept our eyes upon the floor?
Perhaps some trigger deep in mind that woke us up from being blind.

To forge ahead with friends new found with paths that cross and wander round.
For both to touch that sacred place that only angels seek embrace.
To graze the flesh that sends the heart in spirals up to meet the lark
Whose sweet song rests upon the ears of those to soothe their unfound fears.

12/02/2020

FAail.InG aGAain

A soldier in a muddy trench
We watch the film but not the stench
Of comrades drenched in young, red blood
That fall unknown in putrid mud

The shell's thud is constant measure
Young lives slip as buried treasure
To the earth, they disappear
Leave sweethearts in daily fear

Move on now just a hundred years
And loved ones still are shedding tears
For family that is torn to shreds
While bombs and bullets rain on heads

But now the foe has changed somewhat
From expansionistic idiot clots
To sides that are both right and wrong
Who sing different tunes to religious song

As God looks down in true despair
His children claw and spit and tear
He gave them home for all to thrive
But split asunder they connive

Continuing the endless strife
Not heeding cost, not heeding life
To teach the children hate not love
To teach continuously there is no dove

No answer to the different story
They all will die in so-called glory
Please talk and stop the madness mind
For God's sake and for human kind.

16/05/2021 20:15-20:42

A strange sensation

A still cool night
Lit by the stars
Arms outstretched to ink black sky
Each diamond point
Embracing a why
Their ancient light
Looks down on our blue
Destruction and chaos, it's what we choose.
We are but a point in time and in space
A million years is a blink in the race.
Our hands held the keys
Now lost with the seas
Now lost without trace
They're gone now
For the green man to hold
And the piper to play and save what we've sold.

12/10/2020

FeeeeeT

Age creeps up from deep within
The mind, the body, the outward grin
The friendly smile or agile brain
But body's strength is on the wane

The creeping wither diluting blood
The energy no longer flood
An effort to even raise a hand
Strength slips away like wave-washed sand

But all of that is yet to come
For present let's enjoy the sun
And wander now through meadows sweet
While I can still stand on my feet.

12/09/2020

StAt U

AS TALL AS A STATUE, AS PALE AS A GHOST
WITH RED, RUBY LIPS THAT I LIKE THE MOST
THE DELICATE WAIST
THE PALE, PALE SKIN
THE SCENT OF ANTICIPATION I REVEL IN

STRIKING A POSE TO BEST EFFECT
PERFECTLY FROM FEET TO NECK
SLOWLY MELTING TO THE FLOOR
SHUT THE BLINDS AND LOCK THE DOOR

OUTLINED NOW AGAINST THE SHEETS
LYING BACK WITH ARMS TO GREET
A WARMTH AND HEAT INTENSE AND SWEET
WRAPPING ME IN SHADOWS DEEP

HEARTS THAT BEAT TOGETHER NOW
SWEAT APPEARS ON BOTH OUR BROWS
INTENSITY UP TO THE STARS
NO HOLDING BACK, NO EMOTION BARRED

AND WHEN DONE, TWO SPENT SOULS
CAN CARESS AND EACH OTHER HOLD
TO CATCH A BREATH AND SMILE WITH LIPS
ONCE GREEDY FOR NECTAR SIPS.

08/06/2021 15:30-15:45

Fri End

Backs turned, you walk away
Disappear into the spray
Never knowing what was to come
All the laughter, all the fun

You jump in space, free again
To take the car, to take the train
To walk uncaring on the hill
To lie back in the meadow still

The sun, the sky,
The pure clear air
Inhaled with joy and
Not despair.

The smell of jasmine soothes your mind
A friend to you and always kind.

13/06/2020

bEst Fri. End fLo

Big, brown eyes
A faithful lick, a wagging tale
A playful flick that never fails
Stuck like glue through thick and thin
They're always there to help you win

A furry friend who questions not
The command you give to make her stop

A chase around with stick and ball
In the kitchen, in the hall
Up the stairs and on the bed
In the garden, in the shed

Mad days, sad days, she's always there
To answer questions and answer prayers
A visit short in life's rich book
Remembering her deep soul look

And time to go, she breaks your heart
But leaves with memories that can't depart
Sails to the stars and leaves you bereft
That's Flo for you the day she left.

01/08/2020

BRe -AK

Breaking dawn
Breaking bread
Breaking cups
Breaking ground
Breaking up
Breaking down

Breaking in
Breaking out
Breaking cars
Breaking shafts (as in half)

Break for tea
Break for tea

Breaking masts

Breaking glass
Breaking pencil
Breaking seals (as in jars)
Breaking waters
Breaking teeth
Breaking laughter

Breaking chains
Breaking minds
Breaking arms
Breaking bank
Breaking legs
Breaking camp

Break for beer
Break for beer
Break for beer

Breaking news
Breaking clouds
Breaking records
Breaking dams
Breaking promise
Breaking trust

Broken heart

Breaa. THE Breath

Breathe in breathe out, breathe in breathe out
Measuring the time, measuring the doubt
Measuring the celebration of life within

Breathe out again breathe in
Step one step two pacing out the measure
Leave behind our steps for others to treasure
Breathing out our way through paths
That take us through the light and dark

Breathing in our lover's breath
Breathing out another breath
That takes us closer towards death
Breathing in the scent of spring

Breathe out the winter's shivering sting
We breathe our way
Breathe out
Through life's rich journey with a shout
That in itself, breathes out

As we then breathe deeply again with doubt

So breath, you see, will hold us all
Together before we make our fall
And finally breathe our last breath in
And with our last breath
Breathe out.

14/05/2021 22:00-22:15

I's

Crystal eyes peer from deep
Cold oceans in crazy sleep
Look out on a world and pierce the page
Know not what looks back to calm the rage

Or love that's lost in raging seas that run so deep

A steely gaze and skin so fair with ruby lips that beckon dare
The cherry taste of perfume hangs
Clouds of hope within my hands

A sweet caress, a calming touch, to release the fire we love so much
To draw aside, to sigh relief, to hold each other's strong belief
Of mutual trust, of chorus song, we both know now where we belong.

10/11/2020

Lu Na

Darkness now surrounds my soul
My eyes stare into deep, black holes
At the bottom sits a screaming man
With feet in stone who cannot stand

Release is fruitless, there are no stairs
To escape the vipered pit and lair
Left to rot on hands and knees
Never see the grass and trees

A lunar angel lifts his soul
To take away the red-hot coals
Replacing them with soft, warm lips
That soothe the wounds with gentle sips

She breathes on dew to cool the flesh
As cool dawn air brings thoughts afresh
No longer chained, a heart now free
His eyes now open can truly see.

25/12/2020

fLoAAAAAAAt+ingG

Disconnect myself from voice and sound
A conversation circles round

Familiar tunes seep down the hall
Rest on my ears
Shafts of sunlight
Dancing dust slips in and out

Drift off into semi-sleep
Mind wanders, shallow, then deep
Flickering eyelids view the scene
Floors are grey, walls are cream

Soul looks down on sleeping form
Now it's becoming torn
Return to flesh to wake and start
Or skip return and drift apart

Leave the mortal flesh behind
Lying there would be more kind
But there's plenty left and time to go
Now's not the time to leave the show

Feather music washes down
Wakens me with gentle sound
Soft guitars float and weave
Their magic dance, waves like sea

Wake me, is it really me?
My hands can move and I can feel
Yes, I can feel, I CAN FEEL
The warm, glow sun that lights the room
That always saves me from the swoon

14/05/2021 18:15-18:45

ThO SSEEEE

Drifting round the starlit sky
Looking down and wonder why
I'm gliding round and looking down
On rooftops and surrounding ground

I've sprouted wings like Superman
With twists and loops, I rocket round
And sit on dizzy edges high
With wings folded by my side

All is now just black and white
Washed by the moon's eerie light
The dreamscape I look down upon
Changes like chameleons

The dream I'm in, familiar lines
Repeats itself from time to time
Sometimes ends in landing soft
And others crashing through the loft

And then appears just in range
A technicolour shape that changes
No eyes, no face, no mouth or nose
It seems to be one of Those

Where's it from, it's always there
Does it comfort does it scare?
It seems to not be there for me, again
Perhaps a guide for other men

I stretch to touch the billowing form
But out of reach it shifts like storms
That boil and froth in distant clouds
Its presence makes me cry out loud

It's been there since the age of four
Brooding by the schoolroom door
Visiting from time to time
It keeps me safe from inner mind.

21/05/2021 21:15-21:50

Cl OsE

Empty now, stillness reigns
Memory coursing through my veins
Husk dry desert of the mind
Eyes now cloaked make me blind

Evening scent I breathe in deep
Creating soporific sleep
Summer dusk envelops skies
Of orange suns that say goodbye

Relax now the day dissolves
And runs down into unseen holes
That draws life's poison from my frame
To rivers of cathartic drains

Cloak of twilight, shimmers mist
Of dancing fingers that slowly twist
Drifting over honey fields
Of silent sentinels of meals

Warm air dampens every sound
Still now blankets daytime down
Dreamland shuffles quietly in
And fades away at morning din.

05/08/2021 12:00-14:35

hAaapy dAze

English seaside is England's breeze side
Sunshine, ice cream, big beach, views wide
Kites fly (sometimes)
Spades and buckets, gobstoppers, suck it.

Harbour wall, seagulls call
Fish and chips, grandma sits
Kids run about, scream and shout
Wrapped in shawl, cod for all.

1960s digging holes in the sand, don't feel cold
Great big waves, great big Dave
Boiled egg lunch, not my fave
Sandy blankets, Homeward Bound is all the rage

Seas still cold, but some are bold
Now waist deep will make you screech
In the distance, great big ship
Aunts will always take a dip.

See the dogs race down the sand
Jump for joy, balls thrown from hand
Exhausted now, they're all in bed
With seaside dreams inside their heads.

30/05/2021 22:35-22:51

Wat-Er Of LIiiFe

Floods here they come
To wash away the doubt
To wash the lands that shout

Give me rain, give me seed
Give the hungry mouths a feed

Give the lost some found
Give the plough some ground

Give the dust some mud
Stop the river of blood

Give the war some peace
Let the struggle cease

Embrace the love
Free the dove

Give mankind some sense
Help me jump the fence

Stop the train on runaway tracks
Bring me the edge, bring it back

Bring the sun, bring the dawn
Wake me up not forlorn

Take my hands and lead me there
To your heart to your stare

Wrap me in the deep pool eyes
And make me glad to be alive.

15/06/2021 23:15-23:35

ScREEN(m) ed out

FROM THE SCREEN REACHING OUT
STICK-THIN KIDS LIE LISTLESS
EMACIATED IN A WORLD THAT TAKES THE LIFE AND SQUEEZING
HARD
DESTROYS THE CHANCE OF DECENT LIFE OF FAIRNESS

OUR HEART GOES OUT BUT WHAT'S THE POINT
THEY'RE FAR AWAY IN SOME DARK CORNER
OF OUR DEAR EARTH, VICTIMS OF CONFLICT,
POLITICS, CORRUPTION

THEY'RE THERE AGAIN DAY AFTER DAY
YEAR AFTER YEAR, ON AND ON STRETCHING INTO
TIME UNIMAGINABLE
WORSE AND WORSE AS MANKIND EXPANDS
LIKE A PLAGUE THAT'S BLIGHTING
EVERYTHING IT TOUCHES.

THE DOORBELL RINGS.
HELLO MATE
A BEER? GREAT, THANKS.
I'LL SWITCH THE TELLY OFF
AND IN AN INSTANT
PROBLEM SOLVED.

17/06/2021 23:00-23:15

FiSH Sing

Gazing up from ocean deep
Fishy eyes and silver streak
Murderous hooks they dangle there
To the mackerel's deep despair

One by one themselves impale
On shiny hooks hung over rails
Each day the boat brings more and more
Inexpert fishers to the call

Catches they get less and less
Fish hoovered up in deep distress
Empty oceans, watery voids
Of nothing left, just silent noise

As tankers coast to coast they sail
And drown the loudest sound of whales
That reverberated round the seas
The sounds now lost to human greed

Meanwhile our fish they circle round
Curious at what they've found
Thinking food, they take the hook
Like us, it's death and then we're cooked.

17/07/2021 11:00-11:46

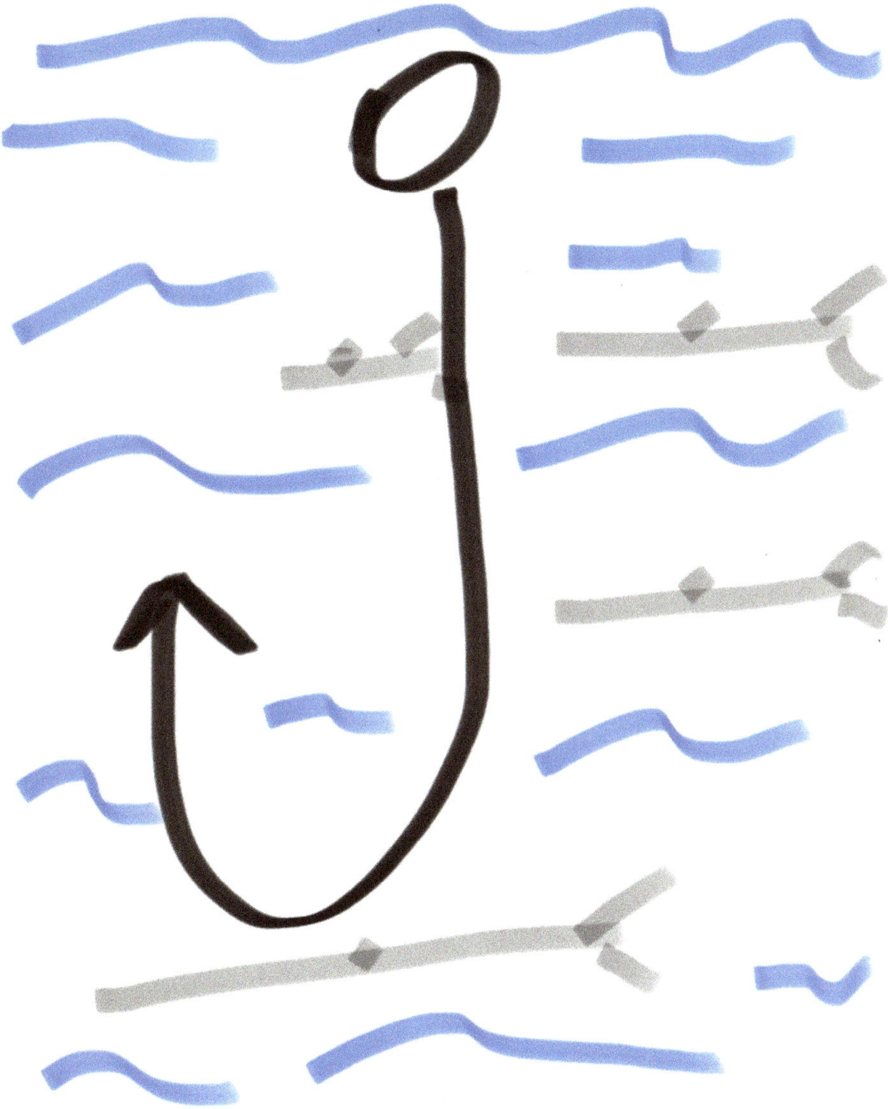

MAD SHADOWS

Ghosts in the room they sit on my bed
They swirl in the dark and enter my head
They stir up the memories of life gone before
They float to the ceiling and crash through the floor

They wake me up in the dead of night
And make me scream stiff with fright
Wake up with sweat that soaks my back
Or cold as ice that splits and cracks

I breathe them in, I spit them out
They make me choke and writhe and shout
Please take them, rip them from my mind
Remove them from my brain and spine

Gripped with fear, I cannot move
Pinned down now by Satan's hooves
Hope dawn will come and free the night
With sweet, sweet air and rays of light

To wash the world and clean the air
To feel the breeze flow up the stairs
To let my feet sink in the sand
By warm, blue seas in foreign lands

Let's hope when night it comes again
It's laced with scent and warmth and friends
That hold me safe and hold me still
From demons who have intent to kill

And in mad shadows, temper dreams
To steer them from those splitting seams
So I can rest in deep, sweet sleep
My secret council let me keep.

19/03/2021

Stu nnnd

HIT ME WITH BEAUTY
KEEP ME WITH YOUR EYES
LET ME SINK DOWN DEEP INTO YOUR THIGHS
CATCH ME WITH YOUR WORDS
KEEP ME WITH YOUR SIGHS
LET ME DREAM ABOUT YOU TILL I DIE

LET ME STAY IN YOUR SPELL
WHERE I CAN LIE AND I CAN DWELL
LET YOUR HAIR NOW BRUSH MY FACE
TO TAKE ME OFF TO TIME AND SPACE

LET BODY COME AS ONE TO YOURS
LET ME EMBRACE YOU WITH THE SWORD
LET ME SING AND LET ME DANCE
LET THE STALLIONS LOOSE TO PRANCE

LET ME SING UP TO THE SUN
THIS IS LIFE NOW IT'S BEGUN
LET MY HEART SING CLEAR AND FREE
LET ME SEE IT'S REALLY ME.

28/12/2020

WHol es

Holes are where we come from
Holes are where we go
Holes you need to hang a shelf
You make a hole to sew

Holes are small and holes are large
Some as big as houses
Some have holes in their socks
And others in their trousers

Where would we be without our holes
To extricate our fluids
Everyone has several holes
And that includes the Druids

Holes for stuff to flow from
And holes to take the cream
Holes that have a tongue inside
To kiss and make us dream

Holes for some to live in
Holes that some will dig
Holes that mice come out of
And holes for beer to swig

Where would we be without our holes
To see and piss and shit
We would all be exploding
My friend, that would be it!

20/04/2021

THOug.HT-s

I'VE BURIED MY BROTHER, I'VE BURIED MY DAD
I'VE BURIED MY MOTHER WHICH I FOUND VERY SAD
I'VE BURIED MY UNCLE AND BURIED MY AUNT
SOME THOUGHTS YOU CAN BURY AND SOME THOUGHTS YOU CAN'T

SOME THOUGHTS MAKE YOU HAPPY
SOME THOUGHTS MAKE YOU SAD
AND THINKING A THOUGHT IN ITSELF IS NOT BAD

BUT THOUGHT IS REFLECTION ON THINGS THAT ARE DONE
OR THOUGHT FOR THE FUTURE OF WHAT'S TO BECOME
THINKING DEEP THOUGHT IS GOOD FOR THE MIND
THINKING OF OTHERS IS WHAT MAKES YOU KIND

SOME PEOPLE THINK LIKE OTHERS THAT DRINK
THEY CAN'T GET ENOUGH OF THE CEREBRAL KINK
THEIR MINDS OVERDRIVEN WITH THOUGHT THAT IS RIVEN
WITH FABULOUS THINGS TO MANKIND THAT ARE GIVEN

BUT MY THOUGHT, AS I SIT BY MYSELF BY THE TREE,
IS, I AM JUST HERE, INSIGNIFICANT ME
ALONE WITH MY THOUGHTS THAT ARE JUST MINE TO KEEP
TO MAKE ME LAUGH OR TO MAKE ME WEEP

THEY HELP ME REMEMBER THE TIMES THAT ARE LOST
IN MY MEMORIES' DEPTH AND I NOW COUNT THE COST
OF THINGS THAT ARE DONE, THAT ARE NOW SET IN STONE
OF THINGS THAT HAVE HAPPENED THAT HAVE LEFT ME ALONE

BUT THOUGHT FOR THE FUTURE IS BRIGHT LIKE A STAR
WITH AN UNKNOWN TIME TO JOURNEY THAT FAR
TO REACH THE GOAL IS A THOUGHT TO HOLD TRUE
IT'S REACHED BY ALL BUT GIVEN TO FEW.

29/04/2021

Piii Geons IN My FrrrIDge

I walked downstairs this morning to make a cup of tea
Put slices in the toaster, one for you and one for me
I heated up the kettle, put the bags straight in the cup
And went to get the milk, to top the water up

But opening the fridge was a sight before my eyes
And I have to say I stepped back in surprisingly surprise
He sat there looking at me with that beady look they have
There's a pigeon in my fridge, I must be going mad

He sort of slumped before me, he was obviously cold
How he got there, God knows, but pigeons are quite bold
Maybe he flew in when my back was turned one day
Or smuggled in with groceries like a feathered castaway

One thing is for certain, he'd pecked at all the cheese
Tops gone off the yoghurts, the carrots and the cheese
How long he'd been living there, no one seems to know
But his wife and kids were at the back putting on a show

Now the pigeons homeless evicted just like that
I would have left them living there, to protect him from the cat
Though his cold and damp apartment had lots of food to rifle
I draw the line at pigeon shit in the middle of my trifle.

09/05/2021

tHe Flig/Ht

Just let yourself go to the feelings of bliss
Just let yourself sink under the kiss
The sweet breath of love, the heave and the sigh
The touch of the angel, the brush of the thigh

Sweet scent of the orchids that hang in the air
The grace of her body
The beckoning lair

The hand on the case with its stories contained
The camera that blinks in the mirror that's famed

And to draw aside and look down at the floor

Or to stare into darkness like never before

Look up to the light where freedom became
The saviour, the prophet of life that remains
And when all is done and you float to the moon

In a white silken dress that flows with the tunes

That lifts the heart to heights far beyond
The agreement with dust and that angel in song.

11/06/2021

SUN

Life is good today
Sun is shining, birds are singing
All is rather well
I can smugly sit and dwell
On garden dug and weeds controlled
And now a beer my hand to hold

Not today for doom and gloom
Or a poet trapped in darkened room
But bask in summer, nature's glory
(Even if at times it's gory)

I can sit and read or idly watch
The birds that nest or bees that flit
Busily from flower to flower
Filling up their busy hours

Smell the grass now freshly cut
And soak up sun, there are no buts
Or maybes, alsos, possibly nots
But just English sun, the best we've got.

16/06/2021 15:10-15:40

BEaaaaan ZZ

Life is like a plate of beans
Sometimes saucy, sometimes mean
They're often hot and always tasty
And even warm, they make you hasty

Soak them up with nice, warm bread
And let them get inside your head
Once bean-eaten, you feel well-fed
But take care if eaten in your bed

Some say they eat them cold
But personally, so I've been told,
That consumed like this though still nutritious
I think that way they're not delicious

Beans are always best when hot
A steaming sea straight from the pot
Re-heat them though, they're not the same
Coagulated beans are shame!

But as you eat them, think of this
Hot or cold, they're like a kiss
Comforting, familiar taste
Potentially not good upon the waist.

26/05/2021 22:15-22:25

mAd sHAdoWs (II)

Summer shadows grace my step
Stretch before me, sun behind me
Giant legs and giant arms
Dance like puppets with boyish charm

Few days bring such playful dance
And when they do, it is by chance
The sun it rests in just the place
That causes smiles upon the face

A moment's joy, a moment's laugh
As I wander on the short, cut grass
Dogs now tired with giant jaws
Great, long legs, enormous paws

Wander home in glowing rays
The sun sinks down with orange days
To close the eve in peace and calm
That nurses us through 'til dawn.

12/06/2021 21:20-21:45

Imp eriaL PINT

Now we are England on our own

Shackles of Europe overthrown

Can we return to pounds, shillings and pence

Will we now put up a fence

Will we revert to potatoes with dirt

To half a cucumber, not a portion

And also now, without caution

Spring, not salad onions

But I hear you cry

What about ounces and pounds

Nineteen, eleven and six. Rods, poles, pecks and perches

Chains and furlongs

Teenage kicks

Where are five pounds of King Edwards

Cauliflowers with leaves

Webb's gone to seed

Two bob bits, three farthings, penny, ha'penny

I tell you where, my friend

The drain of history and progress

But I take comfort in all this

As I nurse my very British, warm imperial pint

That they will never, never dare to take

Or am I dreaming?

12/07/2021

OLd R age (wiLl Owe)

The deepest corners of cavernous caves
The depths of oceans, the crests of waves
The weeping willow, the hardened beech
Are all within the writer's reach

But dark lost soul, emotions bold
Shifting sands, trembling hands
Racing heart and gasping breath
Are all the writer's desk of death

To capture briefly passing mist
That fades away to ghostly twist
Grasping air through fingers slip
Like reaching out for distant ships

Emotions hard to pen on page
Results in heart-arresting rage
Express the passion once felt young
The hope of what I may become

But reflecting in the mirror pool
The old man looks back like a fool
And clenches fists as if in rage
Of creeping off the worldly page

Look right now to see the pillow
Lovers hair draped like the willow
Sun and shadow through the blinds
I know now that life is mine.

21/08/2021 21:45-22:06

tHe JoUr Knee

Paths of life, right or left
Some with joy and some bereft
Some be lonely paths we tread
Some with hope, some with dread

Some friends with us will stay the course
Some by the wayside will fall
Some will join along the way
Others they will lag and stray

Whilst paths will cross at random times
Some will jump and cross the line
Some take your hand and lead the way
To lead you into sunny days

Some paths become the motorways
To speed along
Some paths we know that we belong
Some paths are mires we wade through slowly
Some paths we take are oh so lonely

We start the path of life alone
Turn left or right when first leave home
What causes us to take the turn
The unseen hand of fate, I learn

As time goes on, the path it winds
And wanders aimlessly in time
Then slips into the water's edge
To take the boat to which we're pledged.

ThE PaSs I oN

SETTING SUNS GENTLY SINK INTO THE NIGHT
THEY LEAVE THE WORLD WITHOUT A LIGHT
TO RISE AGAIN IN EVERY DAWN WITH REDS THAT GRACE THE SKY EACH MORN

TO CARESS THE WORLD WITH GENTLE RAYS THAT DANCE AMONGST THE MEADOW MAZE
IT WARMS THE EARTH WITH GENTLE CARE TO BRING US LIFE THAT WE CAN SHARE

AS I TOO GAZE UP INTO SPACE
THE SUN'S WARM HANDS CARESS MY FACE
SOFT, SOFT BREEZES WIPE MY BROW
I CAN HEAR YOU NEAR ME NOW

MY EYES NOW CLOSE TO FEEL YOUR TOUCH
THOSE GENTLE HANDS I MISS SO MUCH
YOUR SCENT NOW MAKES MY SENSES RACE
I FEEL YOU NOW BESIDE MY FACE

A QUIET WHISPER WAKES THE HEART
AS LIPS CLOSE TO ME NOW PART
AND KISS MY CHEEK LIKE LAPPING WAVES
UPON THE SHORELINE OF MY DAYS

YOU, LIKE THE SUN, GO ROUND AND ROUND
TO BRING ME DUSKS AND DAWNS NOT FOUND
TO GREET MY EYES WITH SHAFTS OF LIGHT
THAT FOREVER MAKE MY LIFE SO BRIGHT.

19/03/2021

LloSs-T hOPe

Ships they come from over the water
Ships that carry hopes, not slaughter
Ships of peace, not ships of war
Not ships of arms but ships of stores

We all wait hungry on the beach
Watch ships go by beyond our reach
We stand in rags with little hope
Of grasping crumbs from passing boats

So-called leaders, eyes with greed,
Snatch the sacks we badly need
To feed the profits we don't see
They just don't want us to be free

Gripped by hunger, thirst and death
Our voices gone with our last breath
Disease and war, it seals our fate
And grinds us to a numbing state

But white or black, we all are strong
And mankind will some time hear the song
And one day ships will proudly bear
The aid we need and given fair.

01/04/2021

R Eeeeliza-Be Th

Sit alone in darkened grief
With thoughts that are beyond belief
Our lives are gone within a flash
The race is run, it's just a dash

From birth to death, we weave our way
We all take paths that make us stray
And miss our goals unless we're strong
And join the path where we belong

A solemn day will see us out
To leave this earth without a doubt
We can but hope we leave a trail
To show those left we haven't failed

The world united stands as one
We all stand tall until we're gone
Eventually we all will fade
Like autumn into winter's shade

Our life upon this lonesome orb
That hangs in space is very short
Compared to space and time that's gone
None of us are here for long

But rest in peace we all must do
It's something that we cannot choose
The date, the time, when we're to go
We are denied, we'll never know

A duke or prince, we're all the same
Born high or low, it's not a game
To go in pomp or go alone
We all end up as skin and bone

Eventually the bells will ring
A single note and then to sing
A song that's precious to a life
That slipped away from all the strife.

24/04/2021

sPeEeeeEed

Sleek boat to crush the water
Take care to tell your daughter
Men in shades will lure you there
With promises of what they'll share

Choose carefully those you love
If chosen right, you'll sing like doves
Be whisked along at Bluebird speed
Like Campbell at the helm of need

Tempted not by fame and glory
We all know Campbell's fateful story
Ending in obliteration
Posthumous hero of the nation

Instead explore the slower path
The Baker takes his time to craft
The daily bread we all do need
For health and strength and mental deed

Look to the north and you will find
A soulmate of a different kind
One that's fair of mind and nature
One that loves and heart you'll capture.

07/05/2021

wiNDsoF.ChAIN-g

I'M SLIGHTLY DETUNED
I'M SLIGHTLY RE-ROOMED
I'M SLIGHTLY MAD
I'M SLIGHTLY SAD

I'M SLIGHTLY SEEKING WARMTH
I'M SLIGHTLY SEEKING ARMS
I'M SLIGHTLY SEEKING CONSCIOUSNESS
THAT MAKES ME SMILE WITH CHARM

I'M SLIGHTLY SEEKING SMILES
THAT CATCH MY EYE FROM MILES
THAT CATCH MY HEART FROM FALLING
THAT CATCH MY SOUL FROM CALLING

FLOATING DOWN THROUGH WARM, SOFT LIGHT
AND LAND IN ARMS THAT HOLD ME TIGHT
THAT LET ME SLEEP AND LET ME REST
TO WAKE ME SAFE AND WARM IN NEST

AND SHOULD I CHOOSE TO TAKE A TURN
WHEN LIFE'S WINDS START TO WAKE AND CHURN
WHICH THEY DO FROM TIME TO TIME
THEY SIGNAL CHANGE ALONG THE LINE

PERHAPS THIS YEAR, PERHAPS THE NEXT
THEY NEVER FAIL TO GET ME VEXED
BUT FOLLOW THEM, I HAVE NO CHOICE
THE WINDS OF CHANGE THEY HAVE THE VOICE

THAT SEND ME REELING DOWN THE ROAD
THEY BLOW MY BODY TO AND FRO'
THE CHANGE IS FAST, SOMETIMES IT'S SLOW
BUT WHAT'S THE CHANGE I NEVER KNOW

I MUST STUMBLE THROUGH THE HERE AND NOW
THE DAILY GRIND, THE SWEAT ON BROW
BUT ONE DAY I WILL LOOK AROUND
TO NEW WORLDS THAT I'VE NOT YET FOUND

THE WINDS WILL PICK ME UP I KNOW
AND PLACE ME DOWN LIKE DICE THEY THROW
SOMETIMES A SIX, SOMETIMES A ONE
BUT SURE THEY'VE SET THE STARTING GUN.

31/01/2021

ThE giRrrrRrlL

SOFT HAIR, SOFT EYES, SOFT BREASTS, SOFT THIGHS
WARM BREATH, WARM TOUCH, WARM HEART, TOO MUCH
FAST PULSE, FAST CAR, FAST GIRL, TOO FAR
HIGH SKY, HIGH HOPES, HIGH TEA, HIGH NOTES

DEEP EYES, DEEP THOUGHT, DEEP SOUL, DEEP SCAR
JUST SIT, JUST LIE, JUST KISS, TWO PARTS
STAND UP, KNEEL DOWN, ROLL UP, ROLL ROUND
FEEL HOT, FEEL FREE, FEEL SWEAT, FEEL BREEZE

BRIGHT LIPS, BRIGHT SMILES, BRIGHT VIEW, SEE MILES
TIGHT SQUEEZE, TIGHT WAIST, TIGHT HAIR, LOVE STYLE
CARE FREE, CARE LESS, CARE MORE, NO STRESS
TOUCH YOU, TOUCH ME, NOW WE'RE BOTH FREE.

07/05/2021

Lo(o)CKUp

Soporific sleep washes the day
Should I go or should I stay
In the wake world and the fray
Or submit to dreams that let me lay

In a world of calm and sweet night air
Where my breath is measured
And my heart is fair

Where my soul can sing and I can float
Above pollution and filth that gloats
That stifles the trees, the rivers and seas
And grinds our blue into death and disease

If only sleep could answer the call
That screams in endless fall
Mankind has failed and will I wake
To nightmare worlds of greed and hate

If I stay asleep and do not stir
Then nature will claw its way to earth
It'll jump for joy and sing and shout
This is great now man's not out.

11/08/2020

pAthW ay

Still warm light from autumn's torch
Sun's weak rays filter yellow hues
Blackbird trills in echoed alarm
Float in whispered warmth

Scent of autumn, slight decay
Opens up the hallowed way
That ushers winter yet to come
Meanwhile soak up the fading sun

Dried up grasses swish and dance
As I pass ambling down the path
Strip the seeds walking past
And scatter them in random act

Through the dell and up the hill
Past the stream now gliding still
Cows look up indifferent, size me up
As slowly, quizzically, chew the cud

To the lake now, gentle mist
A sheet of milk that swirls and twists
A chill descends, shoulders shake
Hurry back now before it's late

Blackbird still startled in alarm
As I now take your arm
We wander home, two as one
To start tomorrow as today began.

12/07/2021 20:05-20:31

Re Ach oUT

Sweet skin to touch
Sweet lips to kiss
Sweet hair in which to sink to bliss
Eyes that pierce my very soul
That's deep inside me down a hole

Please someone wake me from a sleep
That's dark as ocean's deepest deep
Please lift me to the light beyond
Please caress me with a wakening wand

Then I can breathe the crystal air
So long denied me in the lair
That traps my soul and makes me writhe
And gasp for breath beneath the tide

The fountain of release I crave
Brought on by hands that gently pave
The way to soft and gentle touch
That my body simply craves so much.

15/12/2020

10 Y Ears AftA

That's another ten years gone
Ten years done

What happened there
I blinked and it was gone
Nothing happened, nothing done

Gone in a wink
No time to think
Working away
No time to play

No time to speak
Rushing to the end
No time for friends
No time to spend

Tunes transport me back
To the start line, to the track
To the proverbial starting gun
To Baba O'Riley and all the fun

Lost years gone in a whirl
Disappeared in a twirl
Never to be regained
We're all wasted, again.

12/07/2021 00:10-00:20

Po(och) rEturn

The black dog walks in the room and leaves me in the cloud and gloom
The January skies are grey, the nights are long with shortened day
Rain falls down as shards of glass
That pierce the soul and through me pass
The depths of winter, the winds of hell
Drive down and try me to fell

The night sky boils with melted brains
And swirls around with white hot chains
And rains down pools of molten lead
That burn me lying on my bed

The depth of man is never known
His heart is never on a throne
But tucked away in black abyss
The key long gone and lost to bliss

The pile of rock seems heavy now
It pins the arms and yet somehow
The distant piper calls out loud
Cuts through clamour, cuts through the row

He plays his tune in distant dawn
To summon nature, this fateful fawn
Will save us all if we can but see
To him we answer, not to we.

22/01/2021

In Tens e

THE BREATH ON MY NECK
SWEET PERFUME CONSUMES
INTOXICATION OF ELEGANT FUMES
THAT ANAESTHETISE THE BLOODY SOUL
THAT REACHES TO FIND ETHER TO HOLD.

YOUR EYES LIKE COALS
DARK AND DEEP TO MAKE ME WEEP
TO TURN MY WRIST
TO SHAKE MY FIST
AT SICKNESS THAT INSIDE ME GRIPS.

YOUR PALE, CALM BEAUTY
NOW GENTLE EYES, YOUR SOFT, WARM SKIN
YOUR WELCOME SIGHS.
TWO LOVERS IN THE DARK ENTWINED
EACH CREASE IN FLESH, EACH WELL-KNOWN LINE.
THE SOFT WARM
HAND OF ENDLESS TIME
CREATES A MAP IN EACH ONE'S MIND
OF NIGHTS GONE BY, BUT NOW THE SIGNS
ARE LOST IN MISTY MEMORY OF TIME.
ARE LOST IN MIST
ARE
LOST.

12/01/2021

In Die an

The dream catcher
Protects my world
Saves my mind from going blind
Awakes my soul to nature's folds
Saves me from the sweats of night
Saves from deep, dark fright

If I wake from lone bad lands
I know she'll take me by the hand
And lead me gasping to the light
Where I can leave my dreadful fright

She'll soothe my mind, caress my brow
She'll kiss me softly as she knows how
The talisman she'll hold for me
To keep me safe, to keep me free

From demons that stir beneath
As long as I hold true belief
And ban them coming up for breath
Condemning them to certain death

From tepees to our modern world
The dream catcher keeps safe the world
To teach us to respect the Earth
Take only what we need from birth.

02/03/2021

EdGEs

The edge of the sea is the edge of the sand
The edge of the sky is the edge of the land
The edge of the stars is the edge of my hand
The edge of your breath is the edge where I stand

Reaching up through the gaps
Fingers stretched until they snap
Feeling for the other side
Feeling out to catch the ride

Sweet, sweet breath upon my lips
Give my senses wild, wild trips
You're the girl with Angel eyes
Piercing souls through your disguise

Rescuing all that pass your way
Arms outstretched scoop up the strays
You hold them in and don't let go
Your rainbow eyes all in glow

That capture edges feather-thin
For men like me to revel in
To slip between the gaps of space
And time that measures frantic race.

20/02/2021

iNfiNi

The endless river
Flows past my feet
The fish that meditate in clear and deep
Gently waving with the flow
Their gills pulsating as they go.

The clear, steel waters glide on by
With no thought of time as seasons die
Through glaring sun and winter snow
The river flows on quiet and doe.

Sliding by with serpent stealth
The river measures all our health
Crystal clear, cold and still
The surface mirror reflects the hill.

Look down into the pools of deep
My shadow looks back as though to weep
For days lost to a pointless goal
I should have listened to my soul.

11/10/2020

THE GIIIIRL IN THE ORANGE DRESS

THE GIRL IN THE ORANGE DRESS
AWAITS SOMEONE FOR SWEET CARESS
GENTLE EYES FLICK ROUND THE SCENE
HER BREATH IS STILL, HER EYES SERENE

BENEATH THE DRESS BELIES HER CALM
HER BEATING HEART POUNDS AS IF ALARMED
ANTICIPATE A LOVER'S TRUST
OVERCOME WITH PENT-UP LUST

TWO STRANGERS, YET NOT STRANGE AT ALL
WHOSE LIVES BRUSH BY TO EACH THEY CALL
BOTH NEED A HAND AND SAFE TO HOLD
TO KEEP THE OTHER FROM THE COLD

A HAVEN NOW THEY HAVE TO CRAVE
THE CURTAIN CLOSES ON THE DAY
TO SINK INTO EACH OTHER'S ARMS
TO SHUT THE WORLD OFF, SHUT THE HARM

JUST NOW TWO SOULS IN WALLS ALONE
ANOTHER WORLD CREATES ITS DOME
PROTECTING THEM FROM DAILY STRESS
TOGETHER WITH THE ORANGE DRESS.

15/08/2021 21:05-21:51

thE PrIOr (y)

The house stands still
Waiting for the change
Empty now, silent and strange
No more cries of babes in arms
Silently sleeping, silently calm

New key in the door
New steps in the hall
First look at the rooms
First of a frequent call

New vibrance found
New music sound
Knock out this, knock out that
New coat of paint
New jaunty hat

Bursting now, it's come alive
Full of party, busy hive
Walls again jump for joy
Too long in shadow
Fading and coy

Now the sun floods in again
With love and warmth, no longer pain
Sits gently down in comfort haze
New occupants to seize their days.

14/07/2021 23:46-00:00

Re FLeX io=n

The mirror stares into the hand
That holds the thought that holds the brand
That burns the soul through pool-deep eyes
That bring on waves of deep-down sighs.

The soft, pale skin that beckons touch
A soft, warm breath I crave so much
To sink back now onto the bed
Where two entwined have given head.

A lifted heart is end reward
For those that dare take up the sword
Of boundaries that break the mould
Of secrets that we both now hold.

From here now on our lives have changed
With memory we both are chained
With happiness and carefree thoughts
That free the soul from bindings caught.

04/12/2020

Four BiDDeN

THE MOONBEAMS' SWORD LIGHTS UP THE WAY
AWAY FROM THE ELEMENT SOME CALL DAY
IT SHINES THROUGH THE WINDOW AND INTO THE ROOM
WHERE I STARE AT THE CEILING IN SHADOWY GLOOM

AND I LIE HERE STILL WITH IDLE HANDS
THAT TOUCH THE FLESH OF SACRED LANDS
SURROUNDING DARK THAT WRAPS IN PEACE
AND WANDERS MY MIND TO YOUR WARM, SOFT CREASE

TO WATCH YOU NAKED FROM BEHIND
THAT GIVES A GLIMPSE OF WHAT'S ON MY MIND
TO DIVE INTO THE SCENTED WELL
WHERE ALL MEN DREAM AND WISH TO DWELL
TO RAISE THE TUNE, TO RAISE THE CHOIR
TO SATISFY EVERY MAN'S DESIRE
TO LIE BACK THEN WITH POUNDING CHEST
IN ARMS THAT PRESS ME TO YOUR BREAST.

09/02/2021

D/ US /t

The river in flood is now on the wane, the old weary beast rests his head on the chain.

And the butterfly's wings soar up to the sun, that melts us away in to what we've become.

I bend my head like an old man in pain, to be raised up again with soft summer rain.

Our illusory life is a handful of dust that slips through the hand of a traitor.

But now sleeps upon me my breathing is hard, the soldiers are coming and replacing the guard.

And angels are dancing with gossamer wings that mirror the song of later.

11/10/2020

ShoE t Boy HOOD

The safety catch is on
But I'll shoot and I'll be gone
Leave behind the wounded soul
Leave behind an exit hole.

The bullet goes straight through
Piercing flesh on its journey to
Its final place within the wood
Its place where all the statues stood.

Where the children played and made their fires
Where young men knew not of such desires
But brave conquerors they became
As they all joined in the world of games.

The fire's smoke now disappeared
That hung in cloaks of shadow fear
The sun draws eyes up to the sky
The endless blue in crystal guise.

I now rejoice in soft, warm love
With no more bullets from above
No more bullets from the gun
Just soft, green fields and endless sun.

27/02/2021

Tri-Um-Ph

The seas and oceans heave and swell
Their fury is as deep as hell
They choke upon our human waste
That we discard in random haste

They foam and crash against the sands
And spew our crap upon the land
Rejecting all that we discard
To clean its self from our backyard

It heaves and shakes and curls and snakes
Its waves leave boiling tails that take
An endless dredge of mankind's dump
That sinks in mud in foetid clump

Relentless pounding round the clock
To clean its self against the rocks
Then leaves us empty twice a day
Returning twice into the fray

The end will spell a win for sea
And doom for likes of you and me
We all will end in distance time
The sea will calm and clean the slime.

30/01/2021

T He Aaad/VerT

The silver frame reflects the girl
Whose body sends me to a whirl
Around the room and back again
Her beauty drives me just insane

Her supple lines they dance for me
For my eyes only for to see
She tantalises with her smile
She tempts me with posing style

With lips that draw me in the frame
I stand outside her in the rain
Wishing dearly to be there
To caress her body and her hair

To feel her sway and touch my face
As lovers with a warm embrace
To lie beside and breathe her in
Like perfumed meadows of sweetest sin.

06/01/2021

FiNaL iTy

THE SLEEP THAT'S SO DEEP SENDS YOU OFF WITH THE WIND.
THE COMMANDER IN CHIEF HE KNOWS IF YOU'VE SINNED.

COLD BREATH ON THE WINDOW IS CRAZED ON THE PANE. I'M INSIDE THE WALLS. AM I GOING INSANE?
THE WAVES OF ILLUSION LAP ON THE SHORE AND WASH THE DETRITUS OF LIFE GONE BEFORE.

I STUMBLE THROUGH BEAUTY WITH SLAVERING WOLVES HUNGRY FOR SCRAPS OF SELFISH FOOLS.

WITH DARK ENCROACHES SOFT VELVET HANDS, I SLIP INTO SLEEP AND FABULOUS LANDS.

TO DREAM TO BE FREE FROM THE CHAINS OF DESIRE THAT TIE MY HANDS TO THE FLAMES OF FIRE,
CONSUMING MY SOUL IN ELEGANT SPIRES THAT REACH TO THE BLUE AND THE STARS.

I SIT ALONE WITH THAT SAME WHITE STAR THAT SHINES ITS LIGHT. FROM INFINITE FAR, IT WATCHES MY LIFE FROM CIRCLING SPACE AND WILL BE THERE WHEN MY DUST FALLS FROM THIS HUMAN GRACE.

09/11/2020

AbYss

The world is sick and dying fast
The seas are choked and cannot last
Our water shrinks into the skies
And reservoirs dry up

We'll soon be fighting over it to fill our little cups

The grant given us by nature's bounty hand
rescinded now as desert claims land

We sit here in comfy chairs and watch our kind in deep despair
Scrambling for grains of food whilst lead rains down in random mood
Whose great idea to bomb the Earth, to vaporise a child at birth?

A so-called power in far-off lands that sweeps the board like child's hands
The fight goes on in endless war, more deadlier than each before
Which will in time get worse and worse, for war is mankind's deadly curse

But in the end, we all need drink
And food and shelter
So let us think
Before we pour out our tea, no one is better than we

The world must act and pretty fast, to stop all this and help the cast
Of this disastrous play, that's acted out each hour, each day
The powerful now must reach down and pluck the cancer from the ground
To rescue civilisation itself before it just falls off the shelf.

04/05/2021

GGiraaaaaFfE LaaaauGH

A BOOK OF POEMS ON THE SHELF
THAT CANNOT OPEN BY ITSELF
BUT NEEDS A HAND TO TURN THE PAGE
AND READ WORDS FROM ANOTHER AGE

IT'S BEEN SITTING THERE FOR YEARS
IT STANDS ALONE AMONGST ITS PEERS
ITS WORDS FORGOTTEN AS TIME MARCHED ON
ITS READERS SOME NOW PAST AND GONE

I DARE REACH AND PULL IT OUT
THE WELL-WORN SPINE CRACKS WITH A SHOUT
IT NOW FALLS OPEN AT A PAGE
THAT'S WAITED PATIENTLY TO TAKE THE STAGE

THE WORDS ARE READ WITH TEARFUL EYES
AS MEMORY CLOUDS LIKE DARKENED SKIES
AND THEN MY EYES LIGHT UP THE PATH
MR GIRAFFE STILL MAKES ME LAUGH.

01/05/2021

BlAaaCK AnD Why-te?

TURN AROUND, SNAP A SHOT
CATCH A SMILE TO BE FORGOT
SUSPENDED NOW IN TIME FOREVER
STARING FROM THE PAGE TOGETHER

LOOKING IN OR LOOKING OUT
NO KNOWING THEN WHAT LIFE'S ABOUT
A MOMENT FROZEN IN THE FRAME
FOR FUTURE EYES TO PLAY A GAME

WHO IS THE MAN? WHO IS THE GIRL?
WHAT DID THEY DO? WHAT DID UNFURL?
HAVE THEY GOT KIDS? ARE THEY STILL HERE?
DID SHE SMOKE? DID HE DRINK BEER?

WHOSE IS THE HOUSE THE BACKGROUND FRAMES?
WHEN THEY WERE KIDS, DID THEY PLAY GAMES?
OR ARE THEY STRANGERS IN THE HOUR
CAUGHT BY ACCIDENT IN A SHOWER?

DEBATE WILL RAGE FOR YEAR ON YEAR
WHO THEY ARE AND CAN THEY HEAR
BUT LOOK UPON THE BACK NOW FAINT
THEIR NAMES REVEALED LIKE LONG GONE SAINTS

BUT EVEN THEN, ALL WE HAVE
ARE TWO NAMES ON A GRUBBY PHOTOGRAPH
TO KEEP US GUESSING ALL OUR LIVES
REPEATING THAT SNAP FOR FUTURE EYES

BUT LOOKING IN, YOU REALISE
THE BOY IN THERE HE HAS YOUR EYES
HE HAS A SMILE THAT'S NOW LONG GONE
THE HAND THAT HOLDS THE FRAME IS DONE

THE PHOTOGRAPH IT CAPTURES SOULS
IT BORES ITS EYES LIKE LASER HOLES
IT PLAYS A TUNE OF A PAST DANCE
AND LEAVES THE VIEWER IN A TRANCE.

B R

Waiting at the station for an empty train
That's full of empty people standing in the rain
Waiting at the station for the train to come
To open my grey, old world to a distant sun

Listen to the doors shut as it speeds away
Leaving from the platform
Leaving shadows of dismay

Disappearing down the line with it goes all hope
Of meeting her and touching her and feeling her so close
One day I might get lucky and glimpse as she goes by
Waving from the window at some other lonely guy

I hope her heart is warm enough to try to come again
I hope her smile is true enough to stop the pouring rain
I hope that hope itself doesn't wash right down the drain
But most of all I hope that I'll see her once again.

21/05/2021

He At

WAVES OF HEAT, WHIRR OF FANS
SWEAT SHINING ON MY HANDS
DISTANT, COMBINE IN FIELDS OF SUN
BIRDS NOW SILENT BROODING DONE

LOVERS IN PARKS
DISTANT LARKS
BUCKETS OF ICE, COOLING SOMETHING NICE
SUSPENDED TIME, AS SUN JUST SHINES

POPULATION STOPS, CONVERSATION, IT'S HOT
MOVE NOW SLOWLY, SHUTTING DOWN
SLEEP OF HEAT, EYES SQUINT ROUND

EVENING COMES WITH MILKY COOL
STILLNESS REINS ON LOBSTER FOOLS
BARBECUES SPRING FROM THE SAND
BACON AND SAUSAGE START TO LAND

BOTTLE OF WINE, A FEW COOL BEERS
GREAT FRIENDS NOW, GLASSES CHEER
SUN SINKS DOWN AND TWILIGHT COMES
THEN HAND IN HAND WALK HOME AS ONE.

21/07/2021 13:05-13:20

GEnntlE -MeN TIIiiiime!

We all are born with a bank of time
To spend as we wish through rain and shine
As we wend our way through daily slug
For some poor souls, they lose the plug.

And time for them drains quickly away
Twenty-seven seems to be the day
That time ran out for those who lost
The race against time, they just went bust.

Time is equal to us all
Black or white, short or tall
Some have time they can waste
Some have time they spend in haste.

Oddly time is slow when very young
And fast when old and clinging on
Time is spent and time is saved
Yet it's more time we actually crave.

Time ticks along in its own sweet way
Year by year and day by day
It creeps upon us with crafty stealth
It's Father Time who measures our health.

Then suddenly our time is up
It's time we went, it's time given up
It's time the curtain finally fell
It's time, gentlemen, please
Oh Hell!

28/06/2021 08:10-15:30

Faaal eN

We fall like raindrops
We're blown like the wind
We're scattered like the seed
We are mist in the fields
We decay like leaves

We fall to the ground
Legs in a knot
Try as we might
We can't get up

Planet in free fall
We've dropped the ball
Earth is scorched
Forests are torched

Out of kilter
We've lost the filter
We've lost our minds
And all become blind

To oceans of crisis
That are deserts of detritus
Fallen from our hands
Fallen to the land

Fall through our fingers
Like muted singers
Waving their arms
To sound the alarm

But it falls on deaf ears
And we're all moved to tears
As the Earth turns its back
And all turns to black

As the final fall is to hell
Which we all learn to fear
From our moment of birth
We've created on Earth.

05/07/2021 20:05-20:40

StrUCTural CoLLaPse

We poets in our ivory towers
Sit and ponder life for hours
We write our prose with serious tones
Of love and death and darkened homes

Of big, black holes that swallow all
Or moonlit skies with werewolf calls
Or long, lost love and painful times
Of childhoods lost and struggling lines

Sometimes agonise with a line
That taxes brains from time to time
Is the writing that profound
To change the world with fist to pound

And when we write sometimes
The words and metre
And pathos
Do not sit very easily
Which makes it difficult on occasion to express one's thoughts!

17/06/2021 20:09-20:37

SYLPh

Wrapped in black a draping gown
Flows around like silken down
Lures senses down the roads of light
Leads me to the velvet night

Hold you in the translucent dress
Raise the game with your caress
Glimpse your form through shafts of dreams
You sway before me, form serene

Tempting touch and bodies close
Waves of intoxicated dose
Dizziness now sweeps my mind
While arms embrace me from behind

Soft, warm lips across my neck
Whispered promise now in check
Angel hands that raise the beast
Before you gorge upon the feast

Now you stand before the mirror
Sylphen body still in quiver
Wrapped again in black lace dress
To tempt me more, to make me guess.

07/07/2021 00:00-00:23

ThE Lo-VeR

You are the girl
I am the man
Worlds apart we make what we can
Of sense in our lives that delivers its blows
To random events that never have shown

The sleight of hand that the dealer deals
From under the cloth where emotions we steal

With poker precision that makes it wrong

To consider the bandage we all put on
To protect ourselves from mists of rain that pour from our hearts with winter's pain

The cards he deals, the hand he lays
Before you, may just fix your gaze
You think you've won but all is lost
As his ace reveals the actual cost

Of separate lives that collide in the night with silent words of comfort and light
And pictures reveal a sensual glimpse of times to come, maybe times to sin
You lie like an angel at rest on the bed, your thoughts locked up for only your head
But maybe just one chink at a time I hope one day they'll be partially mine.

20/11/2020

Dream InG SunS

It's said that when you came to me
With stories of your life that's gone,
You needed a hand to hold, a shoulder to lean against and cry on.

Or was it that I needed you more than the life I lead
A lover to join me in the last days of dreaming suns to sigh on.

The journey this then took us on, around the world, emotions strong
To fight all mountains in our way, to fight the eagerness to stay
Within the confines of our bodies' needs.

Ignore the signs that tear apart lovers' lives and lovers' hearts
But pressing on through stormy nights and darkness.
Climbing over rocks of fear, though weary, we are still here, and clutch at fire and ashes.

Like all lovers gone before, parting, eyes upon the floor
Hoping each contains a spark
To kindle heat held deep inside, to burst out into laser light from the ocean's tempest,
unwilling cold and dark.

Now turning back, I meet your eyes which blue and warm as summer skies
Greet my gaze with welcome, child-like laughter
And walk into each other's arms we realise that no one else will save us from the next
unwritten chapter.

Taking arms we walk alone in silence, minds now sequenced and honed
To each other's thoughts and fears of future moments
The story that you had before entwined with mine we don't need more
Just lovers dreaming suns.

27/08/2021 00:15-01:55

Com Fort

Pale, pale skin to wrap myself in
Velvet touch I crave so much
Like moon's soft light dappled through the leaves
With shafts that dance through gossamer trees

Fading out with ghostly grace
Hide and seek to tease the space
That forms in shadows deep and dark
That separates us from the lark

Who rises mornings on the wing
To call the world
Join in and sing
A dot now in the blue, blue sky
We watch her now from where we lie

We may be sitting worlds apart
But from our windows, beating hearts,
Stretch into space and back again
To call us in from cold, steel rain

For one day soon, a warm embrace
Will let us settle in the place
That makes me smile to all the world
Not now alone, but with my girl.

05/07/2021 23:00-23:39

HeRe WE aRe Again

Universal wars and universal soldiers, guns full of arms, arms full of babes
Unending cycle that never fades

Like pop-up games you hit them down
Appearing again with cancerous frown

Not the last and not the first of desperate mobs dying of thirst

For peace and calm and restful sleep
Not darkness fear of huddled heap

No stomach-wrenching knots within
Waiting to be next of kin

The sickness spreads throughout our Earth and spreads still more with every birth

Ideology splits us in two with white hot lead to pierce the few

Unlucky to get in the way
Or close enough to think they'll stay

Our souls are indeed in a mess
Increasing daily under stress

But most can do is watch and sigh
Bow our heads in 'prayer' and cry.

23/08/2021 13:20-13:35

Old AGe (Wil Owe)

The M(olden) Years
He golden years are supposed to be
That time when you relax
And enjoy the fruits of labour
And sit back with your stack

Increasingly however as I now approach the age
The time I have been waiting for
Has now turned into rage

I thought the golden years would surround me with my gold
But I find now that to my cost
I've great big piles of mould

Mouldy bits around the house
I've mould now in my car
My dog has mouldy bits on him
I've mould in my guitar

My wife she tries to mould me
Into something I am not
But that then goes for every man
I'm afraid that's just his lot

I've a mouldy bit around my bath
And mould now in the shed
I bet if I pull it out
I've mould behind my bed

BUT IF I COULD JUST REPLACE THE MOULD
WITH PILES OF SHINY FLUFF
I WOULD BE VERY RICH INDEED
AND WOULDN'T GIVE A STUFF.

09/12/2021 17:10-17:23

Hunt [er]smoon

September hails the Hunter's Moon
Whose steely light arriving soon
Along with chilling autumn eves
The rustling grass upon the breeze

Blown away is summer's heat
Gone now evenings drawn and sweet
Parting birds for warmer climes
Leaves the natives far behind

English autumn comes along
Slight decay with blackbird song
Cackling in alarm at dusk
Skimming by in deep mistrust

Churches with their distant spires
Strike the hours and measure time
Calling out across the field
A thousand years of fates are sealed

And looking up to Hunter's Moon
Illuminating autumn's gloom
Across the aeons light has spilled
To light another year fulfilled

Of harvest now brought safely in
Of Christian song that rises din
Of fires to warm the aching hearts
Of lovers that to death does part.

02/09/2021

Chinewrde

Sitting carefully amongst the trees
The distant castle gently breathes
A thousand years of history
In shadowed shrouds of mystery

What have these windy worn walls seen
Sieges, victories, a well-known queen
Noblemen that fall and rise
Ignominious peasant lives

We wander round and touch the stone
And read about who made it home
But what about those poor souls
That cut the wood and dug the holes

Imagine standing in a field
Where's the place that will least yield?
This looks okay, it's on a mound
Good place here to break some ground

Dig here, my man, and make it quick
We need to get some stone and brick
Towers 4,100 feet
And walls, I think, thick and deep

And oh, a moat, yes, really twee
Full of fish for Friday tea
A drawbridge that goes up and down
In case the riff raff come around

But seriously back to the plot
The general population's lot
To spend the rest of given life
Building castles for someone's wife

A mammoth task for all the work
The Mason, Joiner, Smith, and Clerk
To raise a sandstone fort of fear
To cast its presence down the years

But once it was a building site
Foundations in, a busy hive
Of hundreds working tirelessly
Stone by stone for us to see

Who placed that large block in the wall?
What was his name? Did he fall?
Or did he work until he stopped
With worn-out limbs and then he dropped?

Its secrets we will never know
As history tends to never show
The minutia truth of daily life
The love, the work and daily strife

But as I amble round the grounds
Remember boyhood running round
Climbed the walls illegally
But now I get inside for free.

06/09/2021 23:05:00:35

sPIT 110ire

AS I SIT AND GENTLY CLAP
SUMMER SUN UPON MY BACK
AND SINK INTO THE WICKER CHAIR
TO WATCH THE BALL SOAR THROUGH THE AIR

NUMBERS LAZILY CREEPING UP
IN SMALL AMOUNTS, DEPENDS ON LUCK
GROUPED IN WHITE THEY MILL ABOUT
SOMETIMES AN OCCASIONAL SHOUT

IN FADED HUT, A GAME IS PLAYED
SANDWICHES, TEA AND LEMONADE
ARRANGED ON PLATES FOR THIRSTY MEN
BEFORE VENTURING ON THE FIELD AGAIN

ENGLISHNESS IS ALL AROUND
THE SHORT-MOWED GRASS, THE GENTLE SOUND
OF BAT ON BALL, THE TICK THE TOCK
I SIP MY TEA, OLD CHURCH CLOCK

THE CLOUDS NOW PART AND GENTLE SHADE
COOLS NOW MY GLASS OF LEMONADE
TEMPERAMENTAL ENGLISH WEATHER
ACCOMPANYING WILLOW BATTING LEATHER

TO CAP IT ALL WHAT CAN I HEAR
A DISTANT SOUND DRAWS LOUD AND CLEAR
FROM THE SUN A FAMILIAR SHAPE
TWISTS AND TURNS I START TO SHAKE

AND THEN A ROAR THAT DEAFENS EAR
SWOOPS DOWNS BEFORE IT DISAPPEARS
TIPS WAVING AT THE CROWD BELOW
SPITS FIRE AND FLAME AS YOU WELL KNOW

SOMEHOW MY HEART IT SWELLS WITH PRIDE
BRINGS A TEAR INTO MY EYES
FOR LAZY DAYS NOW LONG GONE
REPLACED BY MANIC RUSHING THRONG

RETURNING TO THE PLAY IN HAND
TO SEMI-WATCH THE GAME AS PLANNED
HE LOOKS A VERY DAPPER CHAP
FIRST BALL FROM TEA, HOWZAT!

04/09/2021 20:55-21:13

Look Back

The mirror is strange in the things it reflects
As each morning it stares at me silent, yet quizzical of memory absorbed
Each day that I squint at it blinking into the light of each forgotten dawn

What can it hide? What does it convey? What can it remember? What can it say?
Its grey face reflecting the room, mist on the surface hides the forthcoming day

Slicing my hand across shimmering glass to peer through drips that drop to the floor
Leaking the youth of years gone before, the razor poised on the rubble of flesh
As murderous blades scrape the stubble to death

And washing away St Nicholas' beard revealing the skin once soft and revered
I peer to the depths with questioning eyes for where have I been and what was the ride

A hand on my back that creeps from behind, points to the mirror of infinite time
Past the memory that clouds the room where I stand
Waits like a gambler to lose the last hand

Dust on my shoulder floats to the floor to mix with the footprints that have shuffled before
Into rooms full of candles put out by the breeze of life rushing by with time measured ease

The cards that are dealt to us all one by one, by the dealer whose eyes pierce like the sun
Spell out our fate from the day we began, eventually fade to rust, on a table of chance, though unjust.

You've now turned away walked back to the river, I hope you find your own forgiver
Who welcomes the memory that's just been a token, along with a mirror that's always been broken.

10/09/2021-13/09/2021

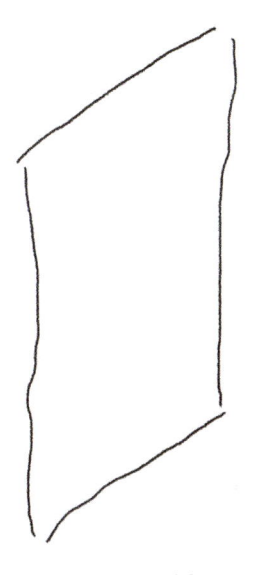

The table

THE CAFÉ TABLE STANDS ALONE
ITS TWO SEATS EMPTY, DRY AS BONE
THE OLIVE TREES THAT STAND BESIDE
IN POTS, THE CONVERSATIONS HIDE.

LISTENING LIKE LOUVRED EARS
IN FRONT OF WINDOWS FULL OF TEARS
FADED SHUTTERS FLAKING GREEN
OF PASSING MEMORIES UNSEEN.

A COFFEE CUP, A GLASS OF WINE
EMPTY NOW AS IF A SIGN
OF TALK IN WHISPER, LOVE AND DEEP
OR OBSERVATIONS OF THE STREET.

THE OLIVE TREES NOW SEEM TO LEAN
TO STRAIN TO HEAR THE LIPS UNSEEN
AS BOTH FALL BACK WITH LAUGHTER CLEAR
THAT SENDS MUSIC TO THE EAR.

THEN UP THEY GET, A KISS ON CHEEK
A WISTFUL EYE AS EACH ONE SPEAKS
GOODBYE FOR NOW BUT THEY BOTH KNOW
TOMORROW'S MEET THEY BOTH WILL SHOW.

AGAIN THE TABLE IT STANDS EMPTY
TO GREET NEW PASSERS-BY A-PLENTY
TO LEAVE THEIR RINGS UPON CLOTH
LIKE MARKS OF LIFE THAT WON'T COME OFF.

THE GINGHAM CLOTH ABSORBS THE STAINS
OF EMOTION SPILLED THAT FALLS LIKE RAIN
LOVERS' SECRET CONTRACTS SPOKEN
OR JUST TWO SOULS WHOSE HEARTS ARE BROKEN.

20/09/2021 21:20-21:50

TAKe & giVe

Is love to give or love to take?
Do I give my love or is it taken?
If it's taken, is it at behest?
If given, is it by request?

Confusion reigns to give, to take, but given can I take it back
Further down life's railroad track
Or taken is gone for good
Lost forever in the wood.

You take my love and lock it up
And leave me cold and out of luck
If given though I can reclaim
And share it with another name.

For ease I'll neither take nor give
But keep my love so I can live
Without the fear of misdirection
I can live without affection.

14/09/2021

2
0
FIVE

Today I'm 25 again, my mind wiped clean from years of stain

Enthusiasm back inside, looking forward to the ride

My step springs with youthful hope, for future plans I don't yet know

To jump the hedge and vault the gate, to race along to unknown date

A heart that's free that knows no fear, the sun of youth that shines so clear

All choice is now in front of me, my mind my own, I can be free

Excited, running down the lane, body free of aches and pains

That age and accident brings on, shouting out and singing song

No thought of actions going forth, but random turns with random thought

Paths to take with no clear end, let's see what's round the next few bends

Close my eyes now, dream away, think not of the next new day

Or where I was or where I've been, or what would be the next new scene

Revelling in the course of youth, look back in envy, and that's the truth

We may be old and wiser now, it all slipped by. I don't know how

Revelling in the course of youth, look back in envy and that's the truth

Or where I was or where I've been, or what would be the next new scene

Close my eyes now, dream away, think not of the next new day

Paths to take with no clear end, let's see what's round the next few bends

No thought of actions going forth, but random turns with random thought

That age and accident brings on, shouting out and singing song

Excited, running down the lane, body free of aches and pains

All choice is now in front of me, my mind my own, I can be free

A heart that's free that knows no fear, the sun of youth that shines so clear

To jump the hedge and vault the gate, to race along to unknown date

My step springs with youthful hope, for future plans I don't yet know

Enthusiasm back inside, looking forward to the ride

Today I'm 25 again, my mind wiped clean from years of stain.

25/08/2021 11:50-12:15

25

sTOrm

Step outside into the storm
The wind it howls as if the norm
Lashing rain, ink black skies
Nature's turmoil on the rise.

Hurricane blows me down the street
The pavement now it leaves my feet
Hands reach down in vice-like grip
To take me on a nightmare trip.

Smashing me on buildings hard
Hurling me into the yard
Breaking bones I hear them snap
Above me gods make thunder claps.

Hurtling now through time and space
Stars strip flesh from tortured face
Contort with speed my cheeks and brow
Lightning fast my body bows.

Until exhausted I lie down
Howling demons all around
Shut my eyes in foetal stance
Save me, SAVE ME from this trance.

Hell on Earth arrives in waves
Brought to us by what we crave
Reaping vengeance on us here
From the darkness through which we peer.

28/09/2021 22:45-23:0

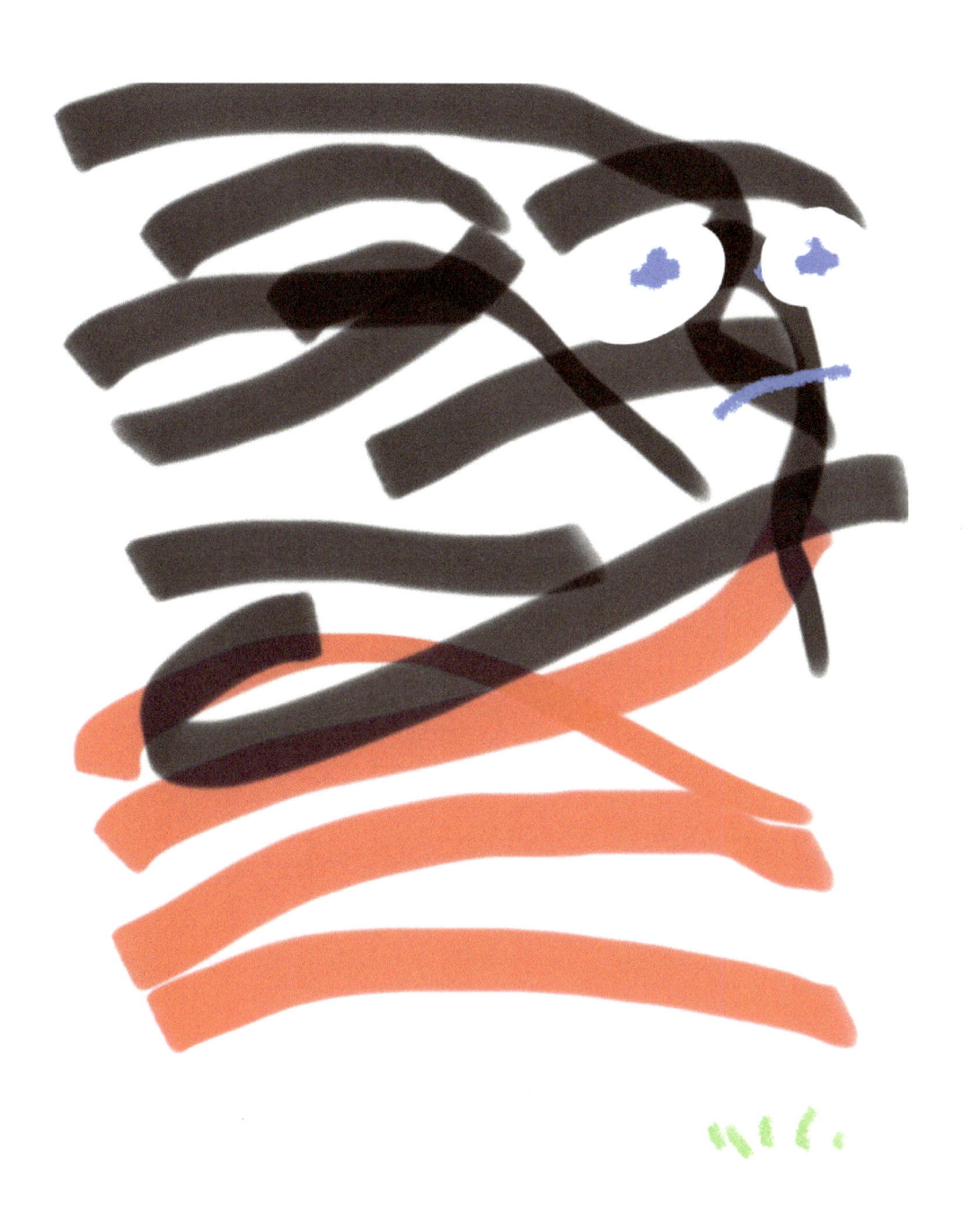

gUArd-Aeons

Three guardians guard my gates
Guide my life, they sit and wait
Watch me as I shamble on
Aimlessly before I'm gone

Protecting me from the thoughts
That sometimes take me out of sorts
Leading me back to the path
Of happiness and carefree laugh

The triangle they form for me
Protects me from the falling tree
Shields me from the blinding light
That sometimes visits me at night

But in the distance on the dunes
Silhouetted by the moon
A fourth protector scouts for me
Helping me to keep me free

His face I have never seen
It's always hidden by the dream
Looking outward hand shades eyes
As if he looks for different guise

I do know if the others fail
To my rescue he will rail
A true, true friend he'll always be
But perhaps that man is really me.

24/09/2021 22:00-22:31

Kill (we're all going to die)

He's white, kill him
He's black, kill him
He's a Christian, kill him
He's a Muslim, kill him
He's Chinese, kill him
He's Russian, kill him
He's an American, kill him
He's an atheist, kill him
He's British, kill him
He's a Jew, kill him
He's an Arab, kill him
It's an animal, kill it
It's a fish, kill it
It's a forest, kill it
It's a sea, kill it
It's an ice sheet, kill it
It's an Earth, kill—
It's a—
Oh sh—

pLOt

SOIL AND DIRT BETWEEN MY HANDS
FOREVER THERE, LIKE SHIFTING SANDS
CRUMBLING DUST THAT FALLS AWAY WHILE
PLANTING IN THE DARK RED CLAY
IN THE SKY THEY CIRCLE ROUND AND WATCH WITH

INTEREST WHAT'S ON THE GROUND
BREATHING IN THE COOL DUSK AIR THE SHOVELS
RHYTHM WITH A SWISH
TURNS CLODS OVER TO RELEASE
EARTH'S SWEET SCENT TO ALL WHO WISH

TO FEEL THE CENTURIES STRETCHED IN TIME
WHERE MEN BEFORE HAVE TOILED IN LINE
IN FURROWED EARTH WITH FURROWED BROWS,
BEFORE THE SUN THEIR HEADS ARE BOWED

MY HANDS AGAIN IN DAMPENED SOIL
CONNECTING WITH A LIFETIME'S TOIL
THINK, TO THE EARTH WE ALL ARE BOUND AS WE
ALL END UP IN THE GROUND

BUT SATISFACTION CROSSES ME AS STANDING UP
AND SIPPING TEA
NEWLY DUG WITH NO MORE WEEDS
I CAN SOW MY WINTER SEED

HANDS NOW COLD, SOIL ENGRAINED INTO MY
HANDS NOW BLACK AND STAINED
I WALK SLOWLY UP THE HILL, SUN'S LOW RAYS ARE
WITH ME STILL

THE LIT FIRE GREETS WITH WARMING FLAME
I REST MY WEARY BONES AGAIN
AS IN THE DARK THE SEEDS THEY WAIT
FOR SPRING AND WARMTH FOR THEM TO WAKE

TO BURST FORTH LIKE A CAREFREE CHILD
THE SOIL REBORN WILL SPRING UP WILD
RELINQUISHED BOUNTY, FOOD AND MANNA
TO FEED MY SOUL AND BODIES CLAMOUR

12/10/2021 17:45-18:25

mIN d

My mind's gone
Frozen, impending time
Like pantomime
Mushed like soup
Jumping through hoops

My mind is pouring from my ears
My eyes filled with salt tears
The condition is infirm
But which way to turn

Which to think first
Earth, hunger, population, thirst
World domination
Or world annihilation

Race to space
Or space to race
Global greed
Or global need

We are but lost
Double-crossed
But who to blame
Ourselves, insane

But one thing's constant
That stands for time
Despite the chaos
Your love is mine.

17/10/2021 21:10-21:35

¼ TET

STRING QUARTETS THAT DWARF THE MOUNTAINS
POUR THEIR HONEYED MUSIC DOWN VALLEYS OF EARS
CREATING RIVERS OF MILK THAT WASH AND SOOTHE
THE JARRED SENSES OF THE DAY.

EACH NOTE FORMING CRISP PEAKS OF ICE
BEFORE MELTING AWAY IN AN AVALANCHE OF SOUND
RACING LIKE MAD DOGS FALLING ON THEIR PREY.

BROODING IN THE HALF-LIGHT, BOWS SLOWLY DRAWN
IN CALCULATED RHYTHM THAT DRAW FROM THE DEPTHS
A CONJURED HARMONY SWEETLY WASHING ROUND THE WALLS
ECHOING DOWN THE CAVERNS OF TIME.

SOFT AS AUTUMN, LIGHT BATHING THE AIR IN MELLOW RAYS
FADING NOTES FALL FROM THE SPRUCE, MAPLE AND WILLOW
IN GENTLE ARCS RESTING AS A CARPET OF LEAVES
SWISHING ROUND FEET OF MANKIND.

SYNCHRONISED, THE PLAYERS GLANCE WITH KNOWING NODS
THAT THEIR PRECISION CREATES A SENSUAL ASSAULT
TRANSPORTING THE LISTENER TO A MOUNTAIN AND PEAK
TO LOOK OUT ON THESE ACCIDENTAL GODS.

05/10/2021 09:45-10:24

PlAn it Rape

Speak to me
Reveal to me
Feel for me
Speak to me over a thousand years
Speak to me over a million seas
Speak to me over a billion suns

Lift me like a thousand mountains
Release me like a thousand fountains

You lie deaf and dumb
Exploited, crushed, under my thumb
Giving up your virgin beauty
You lie numb and do your duty

Defiled, destroyed, slowly dying
Last breath gasping, heart stopped, sighing
Nothing now can be done
You will be left to dust by the cruel sun

But it's in my power to release you
Earth, my love, when you're gone, we'll miss you.

14/10/2021 23:00-23:15

riVeR of ObLiviiion

Crystal waters of chalk rivers
Waving fronds of maiden's hair, trailing like slow green serpents
That shadow the bed where silver trout watch with darting eyes That belie their stillness

Appearing free the river is directed in the confines
Gliding quietly to the sea

I lie back on the soft, green sward, staring up at the blue
The smell of sweet grass and singing waters fill the air with curtains of scent

Like the river, all are directed by the bank of life we can't jump
Pushed forward and downward from the youth of the source
To the delta at the sea where it's mixed into oblivion

But the blue calls
My eyes peer into infinite space, can I see the end
Or am I peering into the past?
The light that bathes me is oh so old

Dozing in the sun's warm hands, squinting up into other lands
Drifting up into space, leaving the human race

Can I lie here forever time, becoming one with the earth that's mine
Or am I pushed like the river
Appearing free to wander but guided by the gravity of life

I shall never know, unless the flood comes and breaks me free.

18/09/2021 10:05-10:25

bRid(g)e

THE JOURNEY TO YOUR HEART
IS LITTERED WITH INTENTIONS
LIKE WALKING TO THE BRIDGE
THAT YOU FORGOT TO MENTION
AND STANDING ON THE PARAPET
REACHING FOR YOUR LOVE
MY ARMS OUTSTRETCHED BEFORE ME
RELEASING ALL THE DOVES

HOPING ONE WILL CATCH YOUR EYE
MY HEAD NOW BOWED IN SORROW
SO I VAINLY HOLD THE MIRROR
TO REFLECT THE TOMORROW
AND WALKING TO THE MIDDLE NOW
OF THE RIVER THAT IT SPANS
PAUSING, GENTLY BREATHING
AS WE SLIP EACH OTHER'S HANDS

BEATING NOW IN UNISON
SLOWLY PACING OUT
STEPS UPON THE PAVEMENT
WE CANNOT LIVE WITHOUT
ENTWINED WITH LOVE TOGETHER
LIKE THE ENGLISH ROSE AND BRIAR
WE PLEDGE OUR LOVE FOREVER
THAT'S FORGED IN COSMIC FIRE

I KNEEL AT THE ALTAR
OF YOUR FREELY GIVEN HEART
AND HOPING THAT CHAINS WE HAVE
NEVER BREAK OR RUST APART
AS BOUND WE ARE AS ONE IN LIFE
SO AS IN DEATH
WE WILL REMAIN AS ONE UNTIL OUR LAST IMMORTAL BREATH.

09/10/2021 21:40-22:10

Un Said

We dance at a distance
Ghosts in each other's arms
Empty eyes staring aimlessly ahead
Steps that follow you, words now unsaid.

Chain me to your altar
Don't let me falter
At the last bastion of your love
That's given like bread
To feed the longing
Of words unsaid.

Sleep, sleep deeply
Dream, dream softly
Paint me in your mind
I hope my love you'll find
But don't forget to shed
The words unsaid.

Walk away from the war
Disregard the battle
Wipe away the blood
Wash it now with tears of the dead
And words unsaid.

Maybe we'll cross the bridge
Find each other on the other side
Lovers parting on the station
Waving in anticipation of hope
That one will raise their head
And speak the words unsaid.

20/10/2021 00:10-00:23

PLAs-sTiCK

THERE'S A LITTLE PIECE OF PLASTIC IN THE KITCHEN DRAWER
ALONG WITH ALL THE BITS AND BOBS, I DON'T KNOW WHAT THEY'RE FOR
BUT EVERY TIME I OPEN IT AND SHUFFLE THINGS AROUND
THIS LITTLE PIECE OF PLASTIC POPS UP AND THEN SINKS DOWN

THIS LITTLE PIECE OF PLASTIC I THINK'S BEEN THERE FOR YEARS
IT MAY BE BROKEN LEGO OR A BRITAIN'S INDIAN SPEAR
IT COULD OF COURSE BE SOMETHING THAT'S ABSOLUTELY CRUCIAL
TO HOLD SOMETHING TOGETHER WHICH, OF COURSE, WOULD BE UNUSUAL

THIS LITTLE PIECE OF PLASTIC IS CHIPPED JUST AT THE END
SO WHETHER IT WAS BROKEN AND PUT IN THERE TO MEND
OR WAS IT A SMALL BROKEN PART THAT CAME FROM SOMETHING LARGER
LIKE A HOUSEHOLD APPLIANCE, OR OLD BATTERY CHARGER

THIS LITTLE PIECE OF PLASTIC IS VERY IRRITATING IN THE DRAWER
AS I DON'T KNOW WHY IT'S THERE OR INDEED JUST WHAT IT'S FOR
YOU CAN BET YOUR LIFE HOWEVER IF I JUST THROW IT AWAY
AFTER YEARS AND YEARS OF KEEPING IT, I'LL NEED IT THE NEXT DAY!
21/10/2021 21:10-21:20

69/77

69/77
Music sounds like heaven
Discovering the unknown
Limited access
To musical axes

Bob to help me get right down
Once a week, whispered sounds
Introducing some new act
Embryonic monsters waiting to hatch

Walking to the local site
Bunch of mates high as kites
Touring heroes to get a glance
Van der Graaf bored my pants

Latest albums taped in batches
Return them (hopefully without scratches)
Album covers read and read
Half the artists are now all dead

Best bands then in the whole wide world
Because I was watching with my girl
Bands have gone, dissolved or died
But the love for my girl is still inside.

21/10/2021 22:15-22:25

Going Undr

I'M GOING UNDER NOW, UNDER THE STORIES YOU HAVE TOLD
MANY TIMES BEFORE
TO OTHERS THAT YOU HAVE OPENED YOUR DOOR
GOING UNDER THE SPELL, CAST BY YOUR SOUL
TO WHICH THE WORLD MOULDS ITS MEMORY OF OLD

I'M GOING UNDER NOW, AS THE RIVER FLOWS BENEATH THE
BRIDGE
BUILT ACROSS THE FOAMING WATERS OF PASSION
SWEEPING AWAY THE RAGS OF RICHES
HELD UP BY OTHERS AS TOKENS OF PICTURES
PAINTED BY THE HAND THAT WRITES THE SCRIPTURES

I'M GOING UNDER NOW, UNDER THE SPELL YOU WEAVE
WITH THE ETHER SO WELL
LOCKING THE DOORS, BOLTING THE GATE
BARRICADING ME IN FROM ALL THE HATE
SINKING INTO YOUR EYES
BREATHING IN THE RIVERS OF SIGHS

I'M GOING UNDER NOW, CLOSING MY EYES
STOPPING THE LIGHT, LET THE HEAT OF THE NIGHT
WASH THE MUSIC'S SOFT GUITARS
FLOAT UP TO STARS OF A BILLION SUNS
BURNING BRIGHT UNTIL, AND AS, YOU ARE WITH ME, THEY
ARE DONE.

29/10/2021 23:05-23:44

Spy derr

You've captured me
In a web I've woven

That I placed at your door
For you to come over

To seduce me with your fluttering eyes
To entice me out of the safety of life

To whisper the intoxication
To vaporise my mind with elation

To take my hand and lead my mind
To bright sunshine that leaves me blind

But frees my body and frees my soul
Prevent my heart from feeling cold

To make it pound deep in my chest
Before I am allowed to rest

Your face so close to mine I see
Your inner soul, it peers at me.

And melting into soft, soft eyes
My life before my mind just flies

Where have I been for all these years
Struggle, strife and many tears

When all I need is close to me
And I hope will forever be.

30/10/2021 21:05-21:39

My Fri END

Walking on a crystal day
The last shrouds of night slipping into the dawn
Distant valleys cloaked in milky mist
Armies of hills disappear with heads above clouds
Of swirling silk

Feet on gravel, warm to the touch from yesterday's heat
As I look down on the silhouettes of woods
Slightly steaming, awaking with birdsong
That floats to senses with the smell of herbs and pine

Morning fire from distant stacks
Greet the world with cracks and snaps

My companion yawns, his slim figure
Slightly bent with rounded back
Barks a laugh as he shifts his pack
On tanned shoulders, sore with straps

Downhill now, drawn by the bakery
Soft, warm bread devoured at speed
Seas of coffee soothing morning thirst
Satiates the body for the coming day

Thirty miles ahead now, the first steps taken
We fall into silence, our own thoughts
Each knowing the uncharted way
As if the journey is emblazoned on future plans.

05/11/2021 21:45-22:05

The (f)EAR

STANDING THERE WITH SHAKING FEAR
AS THEY STICK THE NEEDLE IN MY EAR
BEEN SWOLLEN FOR A FEW DAYS NOW
FILLED WITH FLUID, I DON'T KNOW HOW
BOB IS THERE TO HOLD MY HAND
COMFORTS ME IN WHERE I STAND

CREAM I'VE TRIED, IT DIDN'T WORK
EACH NIGHT RETURNS, BY MORNING HURTS
I LIE THERE, THINK OF NICE LONG WALKS IN THE SOFT, WARM SUN
WITH LONGER TALKS
OF ANIMALS THAT SCURRY ROUND
AS WE COME ALONG, GO TO GROUND

THEN IN THE CAR, WE DRIVE AT SPEED
TO THE HOSPITAL FOR THOSE IN NEED
FAMILIAR SMELL, FAMILIAR FACE
SLIPPY FLOORS, NOT MUCH SPACE
NOW I GET IT, HERE WE ARE AS HE BENDS DOWN AND UMS AND AHS

YES, THAT EAR IS NOT SO GOOD
ANOTHER INJECTION I THINK I SHOULD
NO, YOU DON'T. I'VE GREAT BIG TEETH
BUGGER OFF, VET, AND LEAVE ME IN PEACE!

12/11/2021 18:10-18:45

Ass UMP tioN

I walk with my friend, Assumption

Who guides my thought from the minute I wake
Automatic on assumption, drifting from one moment to another
Assumption I'll wake
Assumption I'll breathe
Assumption I'll eat and drink
Assumption I'll walk and talk

Assumption that you'll be there

But what if Assumption is no longer my friend
How do I function without Assumption?

What if what I assume is now a void, to avoid
Assumption gone, to be
Replaced by my enemy,
Guess

If I walk with Guess, he is or isn't there beside me
Unknown if I wake, or breathe, or eat or drink
I can only guess these things may happen
Like a guess you will return
Not assumption.

19/11/2021 21:10-21:22

A Bad dAY

Twisted serpents in my heart
Strangle emotions before they start
Deep inside the black abyss
I cry for your kiss

I reach for your touch
I miss it so much
Your eyes look straight through
My ghost that's still true.

14/11/2021 01:00-01:10

lOsT HOpe

Young girls are like the spring
Full of hope and joy to bring
Dancing on unwary hearts
That brush the halo of forgotten stars

Joyous laughter, no serious frowns
That grace the brows of older clowns
To catch young men with smiles of glee
Smiles no longer there for me

But I can dream that just one day
I will wake a boy again
To revel in the freedom lost
Through years and years of grinding dust

But watching lovers taking hands
Leading each to other lands
Climbing mountains as they do
Starting loves that are anew

I sit here in my doleful state
Shrivelled skin and bones that ache
Look out at youth as though it's magic
Its beauty lost to me is tragic.

12/11/2021 19:48-19:52

De'aths door

An open door through which all pass
May lead us to a different path
Unless the handle is grasped and turned
No one will know what could be learned

The difficulty of the task,
Of which I must ask,
Is how to first get out the chair
To take the step to free the lair

The comfort of familiar cloth
Has to be first dusted off
Hand on the arms
Super strength levers the body
To stand full length

Step forward into the unknown
Through the gap, all alone
The door that's stood shut and grey
Shut for years cobwebbed up
Barring the way

Grasp the handle slowly down
The latch it clicks, a rush of air
Deep breath of sound
A flash of light comes through the crack
And there is now no going back

A last look back at well-worn chair
No going back, my body's there
I now vacate this Earthly cell
The shrivelled husk of chrysalis hell
With new wings fly through the door
The one we are all waiting for.

03/11/2021 23:05-23:18

s-LasH of rED

A SLASH OF RED
A FLASH OF GREEN
A CANVAS WHITE
BLACK LINES TO DREAM

I STARE TRANSFIXED, DRAWN TO YOUR FACE
CLOSE TO YOU NOW, MY HEART IN RACE
BUTTERFLY EYES
CAUGHT IN THE WIND
GIVE UP SECRETS TO ALL THAT'S SINNED

NEVER ALONE WITH YOUR SMILE
YOUR LOOK OF BEGUILE
CATCHING ME IF I FALL
COMING IF I CALL

RESCUING ME FROM THE EDGE
HOLDING ME TOGETHER ON THE LEDGE
WITH SILKEN THREADS, WRAPPED IN MY SOUL
PROTECT ME WITH THE WARMTH THAT YOU HOLD

LOOKING TO YOU NOW, CLOSING MY EYES
FLOATING UP THROUGH SKIES
LADEN WITH HOPE, SUCH A STEEP SLOPE
SLIPPING BACK UNABLE TO COPE

LEANING FORWARD, TASTE OF RED
THROUGH HALF-CLOSED EYES
A FLASH OF GREEN
OUTLINE OF A CANVAS WHITE.
GOODNIGHT, MY LOVE, GOODNIGHT.

15/10/2021 22:05-22:40

CuP Bored

What lives have been in these cupboards
A hundred years of knives and forks
Bits of string, spent wine corks
Pocket knives and paper clips
Old lipstick to stick on lips

Note pads, pens, pencils and rubbers
All have rested in these cupboards
Sitting in the darkness, waiting to be opened
Staring at the chink of light where the handle's broken

Then one day its quiet space
No longer shuffled into place
But heaved onto another home
Bumped and barged along the stones

Shovelled out into the bin
But oh, what's caused all this sin?
Someone died? A broken home?
Or someone who just lived alone?

Now smelling of a lick of paint
Previous memory now gone faint
New occupants of the cupboard
Note pads, pencils and the rubber.

10/10/2021 09:15-09:35

WIN ter

Leafless fingers reach to space
Winter now has come apace
Suspended nature underfoot
Frozen soul, frozen brook

Hooting owl in the dark
Foxes bark to make their mark
Mr Mouse beneath the leaves
Escapes the claw and scuttles free

Strange crispness, brittle breath
Cools the lungs like breathing death
Clean, clear air that stings the throat
Exhaling clouds of milky smoke

Still, clear night, silent hush
Statue still, no more rush
Reflected night in iced-up pools
Crystal surface, sparkling jewels

Moon's pale finger points the way
Urging me to go, not stay
Casting shadows dark and deep
My progress through the valley's deep

No evil do I now fear
The road lights up, it's crystal clear
That dawn will come and piper's call
Will bring the sun back to us all.

28/11/2021 22:10-22:40

rOOT

Look down at the earth
Long shadows spill from my feet
That shuffle in the dust of bygone days
Clouds of memory skip away on the breeze

Stone in the palm
Smooth and cool
The mirror below, shaded pool
Invites the belligerent rock

Graceful arc from the launch
Motion slowed but no recall
As inertia fails, it starts to fall
Ignorant, the mirror sleeps

Catastrophic, broken skin
The rock is swallowed to the mud
Leaving undivided ripples
Infinite acceleration

Gentle waves lap the bank
Spent concentrics going nowhere
Like the feet that shuffle dust
Unsure which path to follow.

30/11/2021 23:00-23:17

F-EAT (2)

Feet are very neglected
A part of the body that just exists
To keep us upright from dawn 'til dusk
To get us from A to B
To accelerate and stop the car
Sometimes our feet travel too far

Left then right, the endless motion
That keeps us going throughout the day
If we went left, left, left
We would, of course, fall over
If right, right, right, it would all be over

We look at faces, we look at hands
Converse with lips and eyes and ears
We study body language, how we sit
But what about the feet
They just take you to the meet

Look at someone on the stage
Their gaze and hands with you engage
But their feet, they just move around
With no thought to the act or owner
Random shuffles to keep them upright
The feet are always out the spotlight

But I like my feet, they just stick out
The rest of me is up and down
180 degrees, most of the time
But standing up or lying down
My 90-degree feet keep me sound.

05/12/2021 22:00-22:15

T(hE)M

THE BEINGS STRUGGLE FOR MY SOUL
AS TIME GOES ON, THEY BECOME MORE BOLD
TESTING ME IN A RUTHLESS WAY
TESTING ME BY NIGHT, BY DAY

ONE THAT PULLS ME TOWARDS GOOD
ONE THAT WANTS ME AS A HOOD
I WATCH THE WORLD DISINTEGRATE
BEFORE MY EYES IN GREED AND HATE

THE PLAN DIABLO IS GAINING SPEED
AS HUMANITY SINKS NOW TO ITS KNEES
MIRED IN THE TWISTED MINDS
OF MEN WHO THINK THEY HAVE TO SHINE

THE FIST OF EAST, THE FIST OF WEST
NOW FIRMLY CLENCHED AT HIS BEHEST
AS MOUNTAINS SPEW THE FLAMES FROM HELL
DISEASE NOW KILLS WITH POISONED WELLS

BUT SOMEWHERE THERE IS A CHINK OF LIGHT
FOR EACH WITHIN US THE WILL TO FIGHT
EACH ONE OF US HOWEVER SMALL
CAN TAKE THE JUSTICE SWORD FOR ALL

I NOW KNOW THAT FOR HIM TO LOSE
I CAN'T SIT BACK, LET OTHERS CHOOSE
BUT CHARGE WITH ACTIONS LOUD AND BRIGHT
TO CUT RIGHT THROUGH IMPENDING NIGHT

AND EACH SMALL BIT THAT WE UNFURL
WILL CUT THE CANCER FROM OUR WORLD
AND BANISH HIM AS DONE BEFORE
SO WE CAN LIVE IN PEACE ONCE MORE.

03/12/2021 16:30-16:50

Shdw

A life is in the middle
Shadows either side
In the aeons, before and after
Where nothing happens
In the past, we were the future
In the future, we'll be the past

Peering forward, peering back
Shadowy forms drift in and out of sight
The shadow will fade
In a hundred years we'll be a distant smudge
On someone's subconscious memory

But reaching forward there are generations
Unknown to us, struggling through the dust
Of a brief planetary visit
Before their shadow ascends to the ether
Hanging as cloaks engulfing the stars.

11/12/2021 22:00-22:57

bAL-a-NCe

In the end, it's balance
When does love become pain?
When does loss become gain?
When does death become life?
When does peace become strife?

Your easy way, your easy smile
Let me sleep a while
Let me rest weary flesh
Let me wake the day afresh

The balance flicks before my eyes
My ears they rest on your sighs
The half-light caresses your form
You're not the balance, you are the storm

The tempest that enters my mind
The turmoil that makes me blind
You're the angel that calms the water
With the wings that balance the slaughter

In that balance, night becomes day
War becomes play, chains become clay
Moments become towers
Time becomes ours.

23/12/2021 23:20-23:45

close

Navigate the oceans of your love
Crossing the deserts that rain from above
Leading my heart to a life far beyond
Time and space never dreamed of or planned

Floating on wings that unfold as we talk
In delicate whispers that shadow our walk
Our echoes ascend, absorbed by the sun
And return with the truth reborn as we run

Embraced by a feeling that we both belong
To a world of our own of dancing and song
Sheltering us from the storm that rages
Outside of our lives in the books' other pages

Shrouded in peace as we lie side by side
In a shadowy warmth within which we hide.
Protecting us both as we were before birth
From the winds that blow and rage round our Earth.

15/01/2022 00:00-00:15

sEA GIrL

Gone in a whisper, as summer breeze washes
Golden locks
Flowing hair streaming as if the wind is your own

Untamed by your laughter and smiles
Tossing your head in animal mane
The world is yours with hordes at your feet
Conquering all hearts that lay before you

Dancing down the sands into the surf
Sylphen, glistening in the foam
Rising like the mermaids of legend
Goddesses of the mind
Saviours of lost souls
Holders of the universe

Lying back on the green
Fresh meadow of flowers draping your body
Tousled hair thrown back like a cloak
That beckons me to your siren form
Eyes that gaze up to the blue

Drinking in my touch, to quench your longing
Satiated in the embers of your eyes
Quivering at the sound of your sighs
Spent before you, I lay my hands
On snow-white skin that takes the mist
That clouds my sight and leaves me to go clear
To the bridge that hides the key.

15/01/2022 20:05-21:17

Amen

I'm stuck now between your gaze
And games your beauty with emotions play
You arch your back up to the sun
Sensual moments have begun

A peek of flesh beneath your dress
It's causing me now undue stress
Your laughter is like alcohol
Coursing through my body's well

Beads of sweat appearing now
Control my shakes, I don't know how
You take me in your open arms
We press together joined like psalms

That crescendo up and down the scales
Complete themselves in choir-like wails
Amen, Amen, we both now call
Amen, my Lord, take up the sword
Amen again in breathless bliss
Amen, we sink in deep, deep kiss.

22/01/2022

aN vIL

THE BLACKSMITH S HAMMER RINGS DOWN THE AGES
FORGING THE STEEL ON THE ANVIL OF LIFE
WHITE HOT METAL, THE SOULS OF MEN
DRAWN ACROSS THE BLACK FACE
FORMED ACROSS THE HORN
BENT TO CONFORM

BUT WHAT ABOUT THE SPARKS
BREAKING FREE WITH EACH BLOW
BOW NOT TO THE PATTERN
BUT DANCE IN THE GLOW

EACH BRIEFLY SHINING ESCAPING THE HEAT
IN AIR QUICKLY DYING, SHOOTING STARS
A MOMENT'S FREEDOM, CATCHING THE EYE
DANCING LIKE GIRLS IN FIELDS OF RYE

A LESSON TO ALL, AS WE WADE THROUGH THE MIRE
TO BE MOULDED AND BENT LIKE THE STEEL IN THE FIRE
TO CONFORM TO THE SHAPE THAT'S FORMED ON THE HORN
OR TO DANCE LIKE THE SPARKS FREE FROM THE STORM.

01/02/2022 22:05-22:57

eNd of The liNe

Train draws in, lives renewed
Hand through the window, open the door
Step down, municipal smell of station
Journey's end for some
Mind the gap
Case first, bag second, travel done

Whistle blown, slam, slam, slam
Onward change for others
Car, bus, taxi, plane
Possibly another train
Facing forward, facing back
Hand luggage on the rack

Passing stations full of faces
Wrapped in scarves
Men with papers
Girls with pushchairs
Children bundled from the fog

Non-stop through the platforms
Hurtling, rails singing
Doppler
Swan
Vesta
Telegraph and Times
No Smoking
Compartments

Platform slightly on a curve
Sound comes first
Busy people clutch hands
Step back, fear of suction
Black figure, solitary at platform's end

400 TONS, 100 MPH
HERE IT IS
WIND ON FACE
CLOSE NOW
TIMING IS EVERYTHING
ONE STEP
DRIVER'S EYES
OBLIV—

05/02/2022 20:45-21:15

HOPE

I wasn't there
And can't imagine
The fear, the death, the hopeless crowding
The sick, the dying, the poor, the crying
The black abyss that swallowed all
The world aghast the smoke, the pall

Just writing this, it makes me sick
At mankind's filth, at mankind's tricks

No more, forever, we must avert
We must be vigilant, we must be alert
For slipping in around the side
The Reaper coaxes, creeps and rides

And now a handful, memories strong
They speak to us, but not for long
We must remember and not forget
Those poor, poor souls marched to their death.

27/01/2022 22:10-22:38

thE 200,000

MANKIND KNOWS NOTHING
200,000 YEARS OF HUFFING AND PUFFING
CLAWING A WAY UP EVOLUTIONARY LADDERS
WE THEN SLIP DOWN THE SLIPPERY ADDERS

EACH INVENTION SPEEDS THE TIME
TO OUR DEMISE I THINK YOU'LL FIND
WE THINK WE'RE CONQUERING THE VOID
BUT ALL WE DO IS PRODUCE MORE NOISE

THE CLAMOURS OF MANKIND GROW LOUD
AS WE SPREAD ACROSS THE EARTH IN CLOUDS
LIKE LOCUSTS CONSUME ALL
IN THEIR PATH
SO MAN LAYS WASTE TO ALL HE HAS

BUT LIKE THE PLAGUES SWEPT BEFORE
EVENTUALLY WILL BE NO MORE
AS WE ALL WILL EVENTUALLY GO
THE EARTH ONCE MORE WILL START TO GROW

RECOVERING FROM HUMAN SHOCK
THE GLOBE CONTINUES LIKE A CLOCK
RESTING IN RECOVERY ROOM
JUST THE EARTH AND SILVER MOON

BETWEEN THEM AS THEY DANCE AND PLAY
AROUND EACH OTHER'S ORBITS SAY
LET'S HOPE THE NEXT LOT IS MORE SENSIBLE
AS MAN WAS JUST INCOMPREHENSIBLE.

26/01/2022 19:05-19:40

cORt

Catch me when I'm falling
Help me when I'm calling
Hold me in your arms
Bring to me the calm

Your mystery sways before me
I stand in ancient glory
Captured by your gaze
That leads me through the maze

The wordsmiths are at work again
Weaving spell like bullet rain
Soaking me with ignorance
Dowsing me with blackened pigments

Painting me out the scene
As though I've never been
Here upon the Earth
Snuffing out my worth

You're saving grace to catch my soul
Before I disappear down the hole
An inner peace I hope to find
Where we can dance, our arms entwined

Your warmth and touch makes me race
With all my thoughts in endless space
Emotions rarely known to me
As your open arms they set me free.

09/01/2022 00:00-00:38

Con fuse shun

NOTHING IS EVERYTHING
EVERYTHING IS NOTHING
WHAT COMES NEXT?
A MIND THAT'S VEXED

A CLOUD OF IRON
A RIVER OF SALT
A SUN OF ICE
A MOUNTAIN OF MILK

CONFUSION SWEEPS
TIME THAT LEAPS
WARPS MILLENNIA INTO SECONDS
COMPRESSION

WHICH CAME FIRST
THE WATER OR VAPOUR?
THE PEN, THE PAPER?
WITHOUT THE PAPER
PEN IS USELESS
NO PEN, THE PAPER IS FRUITLESS

COMPRESSION IS REQUIRED
IN THE UNIVERSAL CRUCIBLE
COMPRESS THE NOTHING
IT WILL BECOME EVERYTHING
AND THE EVERYTHING WILL BECOME NOTHING.

29/12/2021 17:00-17:14

3

The 5 year old

Eyes reveal the inner soul
Of humanity disappearing down a hole

As lost minds stagger in disbelief
Reach out for help, some small relief

Clouded by the fog rolled in
Shutting out the noise and din

Clutching hands of fragile infants
That follow, trusting, of their charge

Their steps they lead them to their future
The wind is cold the ground is hard.

Bewildered, trusting, of their mothers
To lead them to the arms of others

No comprehension of date or time
But just to stand in endless lines

Gone the laughter of nursery days
The smell of grass, with toys to play

Replaced instead by smell of war
No child should see the blood and gore.

But this is not the first or last

It's the future and the past

As stretched ahead is sick mankind
Obviously deaf, dumb, and blind.

11/03/2022 12:30-12:42

lOst at The CafE

Empty coffee cup
L'addition
Stuck
Between saucer and cup
Sultry sun
Wicker seat
Accordion beat
Another cigarette
Marking time
Blue smoke
Hangs
Like a cloak
Marble top table
Room for two
Blue ashtray
Full of stubs
Plane trees
Cool shade
There she is
Soft white
Flowing dress
Knowing yet unknowing
Her eyes caress
Scan the scene
Pass me like a has been.
Lovers we will never be
She sits alone.
Pression
Sips, sips
Her scent crushes all around.
I chink the change
La Figaro folded
I will never know.

21/02/2022 21:45-22:00

T-emp-eST

I am the sea, tempestuous
Cold and deep
Deadly and dangerous for those that dare sail on me
Foaming, hidden secrets of rock
To catch those unawares
Unfathomable
Harbinger of death, cold, lost souls
Unpredictable deceptive
Endless.
Unknown

I am the sea,
Calm and warm
All embracing, healing
Azure, clear, shallow
Full of life.
Mother of all, birth of man
Unending beauty
Cradle for the sun
Mirror for the moon
Keeper of the shore
Reflector of thoughts

I am the sea or am I man.

16/2/2022. 23:00-23:42

Z s(HeLL) ter

Take me by the hand,
lead me like a lamb that follows gleefully in the steps of the Ewe
Teach me your ways, cast me in your spell, steer me through the storm
Show me the stars, calm my heart, free my mind, free my soul.
Wrap me in your eyes, breathe me in.

For I need shelter
From apocalypse around
From shuddering ground
I need armour of steel
I need seas to hold my tears
Prisons to hold my fears

Rivers to hold the blood
From my ruptured heart
Courage to see me through the darkest of nights
Filled with terror death and fright.

Shelter from the putrid minds
That spread disease like a scum
Enveloping the babes in arms of the old, the young.
Shelter please, I beg, I'm praying now.
A light to guide me from the shadow.

Him and Him now slug it out
But He will win without a doubt.
And as for Him
He will always prevail
So, Against Him we all must rail.

03/03/2022. 20:00-20:20

WaVe Early

The winter is upon us
My father used to say
And up the wooden hill to bed
again, let us pray

Gentle Jesus on my knees
Every night but who to please?
Only six, what do I know
What to say or where to go

Loving family cocoons me in
Keeps me safe and lets me grin
Brother, sister uncles, aunts
Mum and Dad they don't say Can't

Waverley has now long gone
A distant memory in a song
The stairs of terror as a child
Gently Jesus please be mild.

Budgies, white wash, cellars musty
Elvis, solder, God be trusty
Paraffin heater, oh the pain!
Don't knock off the electric train.

Damper in or damper out
No idea what that's about
Muriel she's here to stay
She's just popped up for the day

Dads back it's six o'clock
On the blink the car's on blocks
He faintly smells of engine oil
Hanging from his factory toil.

Summer sun floats through the frame
Kneel on chairs, what's the game
The next car's black, no it's white
I never, ever get it right.

Washing up mum smokes a fag
Between each plate she takes a drag,
Du Maurier's her favourite brand
Slick slim box with Silver band

In the bedroom half past nine
The moon through window brightly shines
Spotted now by brother Dave
The bogey man with sack he waves

Phil now there with slicked back hair
Sharp black tie, blue eyed stare,
To the schoolroom s for a dance
Some young bird to take a chance.

Sleepy now tucked up in bed
Story time to fill my head
Chris is there to read to me
Fills my head with poetry.

These days now are distant shores
That leave me wanting more and more
But with these days I must be,
Satisfied cos it was me

4041 STAR

I know a girl in Wales she's 3 dogs and a parrot

I very well know she feeds them up, but none of them like carrots
She takes them out for nice long walks
Or splashing on the beach
I hope they don't swim out too far and go beyond her reach

They run around and hop and skip, the little one gets bolder
As she strolls nonchalantly on the sand with parrot on her shoulder
Being that she lives in Wales and she's from other parts
The locals can be forgiven for not knowing where to start

Rumour is that she's a pirate, cast upon the shore
Or a brandy smuggler with caves behind the door
All this is unlikely though cos I know she's just retired
And I have, on good advice, the house has been rewired

But as she snuggles down, the fire in the stove
And shuts the winter night out and the waves down by the cove
She's slowly drifting off to sleep but wakes up in a state
Oh no! it's Polly Parrot and fecking 'pieces of eight'!

01/12/2021 18:10-18:21

20 fOUR tHOU (sand)

24,000 suns have set on me
24,000 dawns have woken me
Each one with quickened pace
In one, long and faster race

Dawns and dusks become a blur
The spinning world creates the stir
That blanks my mind as it implodes
At thought that takes me down the road

Rooted here I speed through space
Lightning burns contorted face
As each sun sets it leaves a mark
That plunges life into the dark

But dawn comes round soon enough
Sometimes it's easy, sometimes it's tough
That's 24,000 and one
Another day has just begun

Perhaps there's 10,000 more to go
That figure I'll never know
As I slow down, the sun speeds up
Gazed at from my coffee cup

Which one will I view the last
An orange orb in beauty vast
Or just a cloudy English sky
To which to wave at last goodbye.

25/11/2021 23:00-23:25

Milton Keynes UK
Ingram Content Group UK Ltd.
UKHW051835181023
430785UK00003B/57